Puttin' on the Skits:
Plays for Adults in Managed Care

Puttin' on the Skits:
Plays for Adults in Managed Care

by
Jean Vetter

Venture Publishing, Inc.
State College, Pennsylvania

Production Manager: Richard Yocum
Manuscript Editing: Valerie Fowler, George Lauer, Richard Yocum

Library of Congress Catalogue Card Number 2007921651
ISBN 10: 1-892132-66-4
ISBN 13: 978-1-892132-66-6

Table of Contents

Introduction

When Jean Vetter began working with activity directors of people in managed care, she was impressed by the good cheer and positive spirit of the residents. Though the clients were mainly seniors, many with health problems, most of them shared one trait: They never lost their sense of fun. While crafts showed off their skills, and word games challenged their memories, many especially loved the opportunity to be in the spotlight by reading skits.

While helping to plan one resident's eighty-seventh birthday party, Jean thought it would be nice for the group to perform a short skit. Because it was nearly impossible to find any that were designed with older people in mind, she wrote one for the occasion. It was such a success that she began getting requests to write more and more.

Jean writes skits that give all clients a chance to shine. Whether they are seated at a table in a "Reader's Theater" reading the script, or if able, standing and performing the lines from memory, each performer is allowed their time in the spotlight. She keeps her skits short, using uncomplicated language to allow all members of a group to participate. To help evoke fond memories, she often sets her scenes and chooses topics from a time when mature clients were at their most active. For simplicity's sake, the skits do not require costumes or scenery, and ask for very few props. However, activity directors are encouraged to elaborate as they see fit. The main requirement, and the guarantee for success, is the imagination of the players.

Jean Vetter has written numerous articles, activities, games, and skits for managed care publications. She has written the books *Skits for Seniors, Volume I; Skits for Seniors, Volume II;* and *Heroes*, published by Elderson Publishing, Inc. She is also the author of *Trivia by the Dozen: Encouraging Interaction and Reminiscence in Managed Care*, soon to be published by Venture Publishing, Inc.

Section 1

Family

A Little Moonlight

Characters: Jessie
              Kate
              Miranda

Setting: Any

Prop: None

· ·

JESSIE   My granddaughter came by today and we had such a
              nice visit!

KATE   I remember meeting her, Jessie. A sweet girl. How
              is she?

JESSIE   She's great. She and her boyfriend are getting
              kind of serious, so naturally our talk turned to
              love and romance.

MIRANDA   *(snorts)*

              As if a girl her age would even *dream* that her
              grandmother could know about those things!

JESSIE   She really *IS* interested in what I have to say.

KATE   That's nice, Jessie! I'll bet that most young peo-
              ple really want to know what older people think.
              They need our wisdom to round out their educations.

MIRANDA   Sure they want our opinions! They want to know
              what we think about subjects like their new cars
              or their hairstyles? They think we're just sup-
              posed to give our approval on every single thing
              they do.

JESSIE   Miranda, I'm surprised you feel that way. I think
              it's our responsibility to just be ourselves with
              the kids. Then they'll see us as real people who
              have gone through what they're going through.

KATE   She's right, Miranda. Kids shouldn't be allowed to assume that we were dropped onto this earth as grandmothers.

MIRANDA   Well, my grandkids would be in for a shock if they knew all the wild things I did. Man, did I live every day to the fullest!

JESSIE   Then, for goodness sake, they'd love to hear about your life! Do they know you used to take flying lessons when you were twenty?

MIRANDA   No, of course not! I wouldn't want to give them any ideas to do anything so dangerous.

KATE   And have you told them about the time you drove alone from Chicago to San Francisco to meet your boyfriend when he came back from the Navy?

MIRANDA   Heavens, no! They don't even know I ever had a boyfriend aside from their grandfather.

JESSIE   Do they know you worked as a welder in an airplane factory during World War II?

MIRANDA   No, because I wouldn't want them to go into a factory job! So I've only told them about my career in research.

JESSIE   Well, if they think you spent your life in a lab coat with a microscope under your nose it's your own fault! When did you go from being a fun-loving girl to a being a stuffy woman...when you became a grandmother?

MIRANDA   I just want to set a good example!

KATE   A good example of what—a stick figure? Show them who you really are and they'll brag to their friends about what a cool granny they have.

JESSIE   Miranda, didn't you just say that kids today can't even dream that their grandmothers know about love or romance? How can they, if we don't let them know we are real people?

KATE   She's right. We're definitely real—and always have been. Our hair is just not quite so thick.

JESSIE   And it's a little grayer!

MIRANDA   Well, I wouldn't know where to begin a conversation like that with my grandkids.

KATE   Do like I did. I just began reminiscing about one of my favorite memories. And before I knew it, we were both laughing like young girls. Try it. It's fun.

MIRANDA   Reminisce? How would I ever start?

KATE   Just tell her this...

(motion for everybody to sing)

ALL   *We were sailing along,*
On Moonlight Bay.
You could hear the voices ringing,
They seemed to say,
You have stolen my heart, now don't go 'way!
As we sang Love's Old Sweet Song,
On Moonlight Bay!

(repeat)

Bingo

Characters: Holly
                      Nick

Setting: Any

Prop: None

. . . .

HOLLY My niece called today and said she got a new puppy from the shelter.

NICK What kind did she get?

HOLLY She said he's a little of everything. Sort of a Heinz 57. She's wondering what to name him.

NICK Did you give her any ideas?

HOLLY Not really. If he'd been a German Shepherd, I'd have suggested Max.

NICK Or if he was a Collie, you could have suggested Laddie.

HOLLY Or a French Poodle could be called Pierre.

NICK Does he have spots? She could call him Spotty.

HOLLY No. He's plain brown.

NICK Is he a long-hair? How about Fluffy?

HOLLY Fluffy? No, that's a sissy name for a male dog!

NICK I always had a favorite name for a dog if I were to ever get one.

HOLLY What's that?

NICK It's the name of the dog in that old campfire song...Bingo.

HOLLY   Bingo. That's great! I'll call her and tell her
              that you suggested it.

              (begin singing with Nick, motion for everybody to join)

ALL   *There was a man who had a dog*
              And Bingo was his name-o.
              B.I.N.G.O.
              B.I.N.G.O.
              B.I.N.G.O.
              And Bingo was his name-o.

              There was a man who had a dog
              And Bingo was his name-o.
              (clap) I.N.G.O.
              (clap) I.N.G.O.
              (clap) I.N.G.O.
              And Bingo was his name-o.

              There was a man who had a dog
              And Bingo was his name-o.
              (clap clap) N.G.O.
              (clap clap) N.G.O.
              (clap clap) N.G.O.
              And Bingo was his name-o.

              There was a man who had a dog
              And Bingo was his name-o.
              (clap clap clap) G.O.
              (clap clap clap) G.O.
              (clap clap clap) G.O.
              And Bingo was his name-o.

              There was a man who had a dog
              And Bingo was his name-o.
              (clap clap clap clap) O.
              (clap clap clap clap) O.
              (clap clap clap clap) O.
              And Bingo was his name-o.

              There was a man who had a dog
              And Bingo was his name-o.
              (clap clap clap clap clap)
              (clap clap clap clap clap)
              (clap clap clap clap clap)
              And Bingo was his name-o.

Generation Gap

Characters: Grandma
              Grandpa
              Scott

Setting: The social room at Retirement Village

Prop: A gift-wrapped music CD

. . . .

GRANDPA   Good luck at college, Scott. Now remember, if you ever need anything, call us and we'll help you if we can.

SCOTT   Thanks, Grandpa. I really appreciate that. But I'll be fine.

GRANDMA   We know you will be. You'll meet new friends and you'll be part of the college life in no time.

GRANDPA   What about that girl you were dating last summer, Scott? Will you be writing to her?

SCOTT   No. That's over. It's yesterday's newspaper!

GRANDMA   Well, in a way it's best for you to finish college before you get serious about a girl. You need time to study and just have fun right now.

GRANDPA   Which reminds me, we bought you a little going away present.

              (hands Scott a gift-wrapped CD)

SCOTT   *(unwraps CD)*

              A CD! Why, thanks Grandpa. How did you guys know that I like the CyberDelics?

GRANDMA   Actually, a man at the music store told us that this is a number one hit, so we bought it.

SCOTT   You guys rock.

GRANDPA   *(laughs)*

We try.

GRANDMA   Speaking of rock, just going to the music store
reminded me of when we were your age, Scott. Rock
and roll was just getting started.

SCOTT   Grandma, you're putting me on! Rock and roll can't
be that old!

GRANDMA   *(raises eyebrows)*

Well, I hate to be the one to break the news dear,
but it is! Elvis Presley became popular in the
early fifties. You do the math.

GRANDPA   That's right, Scott. Your Grandma and I danced to
his records when we were dating.

GRANDMA   We bought all his records, too. Rock and roll,
rhythm and blues...we bought them all.

SCOTT   *(looks embarrassed)*

I...I...uh...look, Grandma, I didn't mean...

GRANDMA   *(smiles)*

I know. It's OK.

GRANDPA   And when "Blue Suede Shoes" got popular, I bought
myself a pair.

GRANDMA   You must have known your Grandpa played lead gui-
tar in a rock band, didn't you Scott?

SCOTT   Well, I've always known Grandpa could play. But I
never really thought much about it until now. I
mean, you Grandpa! You were in a rock band?

GRANDPA   *(laughs)*

Yeah, and I was pretty hot, too. We had gigs all
over the East Coast. We even had a fan club.

GRANDMA   *(looks proud)*

And a few groupies too, I might add. Some of them followed the band everywhere they went.

GRANDPA   Well, I married the prettiest one, didn't I, dear?

SCOTT   Grandma, you?! A groupie?!

GRANDMA   You know what? I think we've all been entirely too busy to really get to know each other. The next time this family gets together we have to take the time to talk. Really talk!

SCOTT   *(looks at CD, shakes head)*

That's for sure, Grandma. That's for sure!

Granny From the Black Lagoon

Characters: Teen #1
              Teen #2
              Teen #3
              Mrs. Granger

Setting: Front porch of Mrs. Granger's house

Prop: Bowl of candy

. . . .

TEEN #1   *(knocks on door)*

               Trick or Treat!

TEEN #2   Come on lady, come on, answer the door! We don't got all night.

TEEN #3   Man, whoever lives here is slow!

TEEN #1   You'd be slow too if you were a hundred and twenty-two, like this lady is.

TEEN #2   You know who lives here? And you think she's that old?

TEEN #1   Sure, everybody knows this is where The Granny from the Black Lagoon lives. She's older than the universe.

TEEN #3   Oh yeah? Then she's probably down at the lagoon spooking the alligators.

TEEN #2   How'd they start calling her The Granny from the Black Lagoon?

TEEN #1   Some kids who lived next door to her used to go in her yard and break her flowers. She chased them away, so they got mad and called her that name. It just stuck, I guess.

TEEN #2   Well, I don't see any flowers around here. Just a lot of overgrown bushes and the yard is full of weeds.

TEEN #3	Shhh. I hear somebody coming...and the door's opening...
ALL	Trick or Treat!
MRS. GRANGER	Hello, boys. Help yourself to the candy. What are you dressed up as?
TEEN #1	I'm Spider-man.
TEEN #2	I'm Superman.
TEEN #3	I'm Batman.
MRS. GRANGER	*(smiles)* It's nice to meet three superheroes. I'm The Granny from the Black Lagoon.
TEEN #1	*(gasps)* You're...what?
MRS. GRANGER	Yep. I just got back from spooking a few alligators down at the lagoon.
TEEN #3	*(looks skeptical)* OK. You got us cold. But...how?
MRS. GRANGER	*(points up)* Ha, ha, did you ever hear of a surveillance camera with audio?
TEEN #1	Well, I apologize for that. We wouldn't have said those things if...
MRS. GRANGER	If you knew I was listening? Oh, well, don't worry about it. But seriously, about my bushes needing trimming...

TEEN #2   I apologize for that, too. Really, we were just
               out having fun.

MRS.
GRANGER   Oh, I know that. And I've been looking for some-
               body to trim them for some time now. Would you
               boys be interested in helping me with my yard
               work? I pay pretty well.

TEEN #1   Well, sure. I'll help with the yard.

TEEN #2   Me too.

TEEN #3   I will too. Maybe we could stop by after school
               tomorrow and give you a hand.

MRS.
GRANGER   That would be a big help to me, boys. I'd like to
               get the yard all trimmed and ready for winter.

TEEN #1   OK. Tomorrow. Is after school OK?

MRS.
GRANGER   OK.

               (holds out bowl)

               Have another piece of candy. And, Happy Halloween
               to all of you.

TEEN #2   Happy Halloween.

It's Cool To Be Hot (version 1)

Characters: Edna
              Shelley

Setting: The social room

Prop: None

....

EDNA   Have you heard from your grandson since he started college, Shelley?

SHELLEY   Yes. I was over at my daughter's house when he phoned last weekend so I had a chance to talk to him for a while.

EDNA   How's he doing?

SHELLEY   Well, he told me his school is baaaaaad.

EDNA   Bad? That's awful. Do you think he will adjust to it?

SHELLEY   Oh, I'd say he's already adjusted. He didn't tell me his school is bad, he said it's baaaaaad! There's a big difference.

EDNA   OK. I'm puzzled.

SHELLEY   I was too, for a minute. But then, do you remember when we were that age?

EDNA   Oh, I get it. He's picked up slang. That's normal.

SHELLEY   Right. When we thought a guy was really cool, we said he was hot.

EDNA   And when we thought a song was hot, we said "That's cool."

SHELLEY   *(laugh)*

              Right again. But we have to be careful. I told him that I understood his expressions perfectly well, and he cautioned me against being a dandy lion.

EDNA   Is that someone who tries too hard to be cool...or hot...or whatever?

SHELLEY   Yes. But I think he mostly wants me to be a grandma, not a with-it chick.

EDNA   Ha! I doubt that. He's just pretending because he must know you pretty well by now. But, if you insist, I won't tell your secret.

SHELLEY   My secret?

EDNA   Yes. That you're actually a very with-it chick. He'll find out soon enough on his own.

SHELLEY   Edna, do you know that you're a real baaaaad friend?

EDNA   Aw, go on, Shelley! You're sounding like a dandy lion.

It's Cool To Be Hot (version 2)

Characters: Edna
              Shelley

Setting: The social room

Prop: None

. . . .

EDNA   Have you heard from your grandson since he started college, Shelley?

SHELLEY   Yes. I was over at my daughter's house when he phoned last weekend. So I had a chance to talk to him for a while.

EDNA   How's he doing?

SHELLEY   Well, he told me his school is da bomb.

EDNA   Oh my, that's awful! Did they catch who did it? Was anybody hurt?

SHELLEY   No, no, no. He means that it's very good. "Da bomb" is an expression. A few years ago my oldest granddaughter said her school was "bad" which, of course, meant it was "good."

EDNA   OK. I'm puzzled.

SHELLEY   I was too, for a minute. But then, do you remember when we were that age?

EDNA   Oh, I get it. He's picked up slang. That's normal.

SHELLEY   Right. When we thought a guy was really cool, we said he was hot.

EDNA   And when we thought a song was hot, we said "That's cool."

SHELLEY   (laughs)

              Right again. But we have to be careful. I told him

that I understood his expressions perfectly well, and he just grinned and said I was pretty phat for a grandma.

EDNA   Goodness, why would he say such a terrible thing? You look fit as a fiddle!

SHELLEY   *(smiles)*

Well, I did a little sleuthing, and sure enough, "phat" (this one is spelled P-H-A-T) actually means very cool. But I think he mostly wants me to be a grandma, not some with-it chick.

EDNA   Yes, that's probably true. However, you really *ARE* a with-it chick. It's good that he knows that at his age.

SHELLEY   Edna, do you know that you're a real "phat" friend?

EDNA   *(gives a wary look and smiles)*

For the sake and safety of present company, I'm going to take that as a compliment.

SHELLEY   *(whispers)*

Awesome, dudette.

EDNA   Beg your pardon...

SHELLEY   *(smiles)*

Oh, nothing.

Pretty Bubbles

Characters: Alan
              Dave
              Shirley

Setting: The social room at Briar Lane Senior Home

Prop: None

. . . .

ALAN   *(looks out window)*

              What a dark day! Weather like this gets me down.

SHIRLEY   Me too.

DAVE   But I've heard that by saying we feel a certain
              way, we begin to feel that way.

ALAN   Oh? Like if I say the sun is shining, it's going
              to shine?

DAVE   No. It doesn't work with anything except our-
              selves.

ALAN   So, am I supposed to tell a lie and say it's a
              bright day?

DAVE   No. We can't change the day.

ALAN   Well, dark days get me down.

SHIRLEY   OK, Dave, I'll play along with you. I'll just ignore
              the dark day and tell myself that I feel terrific.

DAVE   That's a good start. Now, think of something that
              really does make you feel terrific.

SHIRLEY   *(smiles)*

              Watching those kids next door when they play.

DAVE   What do they do that makes you feel good, Shirley?

SHIRLEY   Everything. They're so full of fun. They turn everything into a game.

ALAN   They're kids, Shirley. Kids do that.

SHIRLEY   I know. That's why I like to watch them. If they fall down, they just get up and keep on playing. And they don't stop for dark days, either.

ALAN   Well, kids lives are simple. All they have to think about is having fun.

SHIRLEY   Oh, they have their problems, Alan. Just growing up is a big responsibility.

ALAN   Yeah, I guess they do. My big problem when I was a kid was I never had enough time to do all the things I wanted to do.

DAVE   What did you like to do as a kid, Alan?

ALAN   Everything from sports to Cops and Robbers to playing in the marching band.

SHIRLEY   Hopscotch?

ALAN   Sure. And riding my bike. And skateboarding.

SHIRLEY   Church?

ALAN   Couldn't wait for it to be over so I could go out and play.

SHIRLEY   Me too. I loved playing "house" and making a fort and blowing bubbles.

DAVE   Singing?

ALAN   Singing was fun.

DAVE   Then how about singing about bubbles?

ALAN   Huh?

DAVE *(starts singing, motions for all to join in)*

ALL *I'm forever blowing bubbles,*
Pretty bubbles in the air.
They fly so high,
Nearly reach the sky,
Then like my dreams they fade and die.
Fortune's always hiding,
I've looked everywhere.
I'm forever blowing bubbles,
Pretty bubbles in the air.

ALAN *(smiles)*

OK, Dave. You made your point.

SHIRLEY *(leads everybody in another round of the song)*

Smooth Operator

Characters: Tom
              Madeline
              Carl

Setting: Any

Prop: None

. . . .

TOM   How's your granddaughter doing since she moved to
              New York, Madeline?

MADELINE   I talked to her yesterday. She said she loves hav-
              ing her own apartment.

CARL   That's a big step for a girl. Is she finding out
              that things are a lot different than when she was
              living at home?

MADELINE   I'll say. She said she's learned how to organize
              her time so she can get her groceries bought and
              her laundry washed and put away.

TOM   That first year away from home is exciting. And a
              little scary.

CARL   When I first left my parents' house, my problem
              was remembering to set the alarm clock so I could
              get to work on time.

MADELINE   *(laughs)*

              She said she appreciates her father more. Now that
              he isn't there to help with her car, she had to
              have the oil changed herself.

TOM   It sounds like she's doing OK. Does she have a
              boyfriend there yet?

MADELINE   Not really. One man actually asked her, "What is a
              nice girl like you doing in a city like this?"

(laughs)

Talk about an original pick up line!

CARL   Hey, he probably thought he was a smooth operator!

TOM   It's not easy for a guy to ask a girl out. I know. I used to make lists of clever things to say when I met one.

MADELINE   Why do men seem to think girls want to meet glib-talking men?

CARL   Maybe some guys are just unsure of themselves. I know I was.

TOM   You were unsure of yourself? Well, that's a surprise!

CARL   Seriously, I was.

MADELINE   But you play piano. Didn't that give you confidence?

CARL   Sure, I was confident...when I was playing. Talking to a girl was something else.

MADELINE   What do you mean?

CARL   Well, once when I was playing, a girl asked what my favorite song was.

MADELINE   Well, that's good. What did you tell her?

CARL   I just started playing the first one that came to mind. It made me sound like I planned to be a failure.

TOM   What was the song?

CARL   Promise you won't laugh?

MADELINE   Promise.

CARL   "I Can't Give You Anything But Love."

MADELINE   *(laughs)*

Good grief. The words every girl wants to hear!

CARL   Right. You never saw a girl leave so fast in your life.

TOM   Well, I hope that girl found a rich guy who made her very happy.

MADELINE   So do I. And since nobody here is looking for a date, let's sing it.

(begins singing, and motions all to join in)

ALL   *I can't give you anything but love, Baby.*
That's the only thing I've plenty of, Baby.
Dream a while, scheme a while, we're sure to find,
Happiness, and I guess, all those things you've always pined for.

Gee I'd like to see you looking swell, Baby.
Diamond bracelets Woolworth's doesn't sell, Baby.
'Till that lucky day, you know darned well, Baby,
I can't give you anything but love.

Section 2

Patriotic

Freedom Is Not Free

Characters: The Governor
             The State Senator

Setting: Any American city on Veteran's Day

Prop: American Flag

. . . .

GOVERNOR *(addresses crowd)*

> November 11 was originally called Armistice Day,
> to celebrate the day that World War I ended. It
> was later changed to Veteran's Day to honor all
> the veterans of all our wars.

SENATOR The flag displayed here represents everything our
country stands for. It honors the many people who
gave their time, their efforts, and their lives to
protect this nation of ours.

GOVERNOR We're here to remind everyone that the freedoms we
enjoy did not happen by chance. Our freedoms were
paid for with the blood and the lives of millions
of brave men and women.

SENATOR Our country is young compared to many others. Our
founding fathers started out with high ideals and
succeeding generations have built on them.

GOVERNOR The veterans of all of our wars fought to defend
the principles we hold dear.

SENATOR Our veterans are from families that came here from
every corner of the world.

GOVERNOR Every day, more people come to this country to
begin new lives and to take advantage of the life
our veterans have earned for all of us.

SENATOR   But America's uniforms are worn by the individual, not his background. The uniform does not know if its wearer's name begins with Mc or ends with ski.

GOVERNOR   This unified nation owes gratitude to the men and women who have defended it.

SENATOR   So, today, the entire country joins in saying a heartfelt "Thank You" to the veterans of the United States of America.

GOVERNOR   And as a way of saying "thanks" to our veterans, will everybody please join us in singing "You're A Grand Old Flag" by George M. Cohan.

ALL   *You're a grand old flag, you're a high flying flag;*
               And forever in peace, may you wave.
               You're the emblem of the land I love,
               The home of the free and the brave.
               Every heart beats true, under Red, White and Blue,
               Where there's never a boast or brag,
               Should auld acquaintance be forgot,
               Keep your eye on the grand old flag.

Let Freedom Ring

Characters: Larry, a veteran
              Bruno, a veteran
              Ethel, a resident
              Doreen, a resident

Setting: All the residents are gathered on the front lawn for a
              patriotic party.

Prop: Flag

. . . .

LARRY   Ladies and Gentlemen: To begin our celebration,
              we're going to ask Bruno to present the colors for
              us. Bruno, will you do the honors?

              (holds out flag to Bruno)

BRUNO   *(salutes smartly, takes flag and holds it high)*

LARRY   Old Glory is a symbol of everything our country
              has stood for since it was founded in 1776.

BRUNO   This flag represents our people from all walks of
              life, from the most powerful to the most humble.

LARRY   It reminds us of the ones who were here before us.
              The patriots who gave their time in our military
              and the patriots who also served by supporting
              them from the home front.

ETHEL   And the explorers and the settlers.

DOREEN   The bridge builders, the scientists, the miners,
              the truckers.

ETHEL   The mothers, the fathers, the believers, the
              doubters.

DOREEN   The young, the old.

BRUNO   We see our flag today against a cloudless blue sky. But it has survived dark skies, storms, gales, and the smoke of battle.

DOREEN   It is the flag of the people who were born here and the ones who suffered hardships to get here.

ETHEL   It flies for those of us who cherish it and even the ones who don't.

DOREEN   This flag waving freely in the breeze stands for the highest ideals of mankind, spelled out in our Constitution.

BRUNO   It stands for the United States of America.

LARRY   And we would be happy for you to join us in singing the song written in her honor.

ALL   *My country, 'tis of thee, Sweet land of liberty,*
Of thee I sing.
Land where my fathers died, Land of the pilgrims' pride,
From every mountain side, Let freedom ring.

My native country, thee, Land of the noble free,
Thy name I love:
I love the rocks and rills
Thy woods and templed hills:
My heart with rapture thrills, Like that above.

Let music swell the breeze, and ring from all the trees,
Sweet freedom's song.
Let mortal tongues awake, Let all that breathe partake,
Let rocks their silence break, The sound prolong.

Our fathers' God, to thee, Author of liberty,
To thee we sing:
Long may our land be bright, with freedom's holy light;
Protect us with thy might, Great God our King.

Only Old Folks Vote

Characters: Jeff
               Scott
               Maureen
               Ina

Setting: The social room, watching election returns

Prop: A magazine with a copy of "Hail to the Chief" tucked
               inside.

. . . .

JEFF   Today while I walking over to the voting booth,
               I saw a young guy with a tee shirt on that said,
               "Only Old Folks Vote."

MAUREEN   Smart Aleck! Maybe he'd like for somebody to tell
               him they're passing a law that says, "Only Old
               Folks Will Be Allowed To Vote."

INA   He'd probably change his tune real quick then.

MAUREEN   Yes, he'd probably start a voter registration cam-
               paign among his friends.

SCOTT   Did you say anything to him?

JEFF   Yeah, I told him to give Stalin that shirt.

MAUREEN   Did he answer you back?

JEFF   He just shrugged and said "Who's Stalin?"

INA   I wouldn't argue with somebody like that. I just
               chalk it up to youthful ignorance.

JEFF   Well, when I was his youthful age, I was serving
               on a submarine in the Pacific.

SCOTT   And you were serving to defend your country's con-
               stitution, weren't you?

JEFF	You bet I was.
SCOTT	*(sadly)*
	Then, I guess you were also serving to protect his First Amendment right to free speech.
JEFF	If I'd have known that's what I was doing, I might not have gone.
MAUREEN	If it's any consolation to you, Jeff, that guy would be the first to claim "constitutional freedom" if you tried to take away his right to free expression.
INA	On a lighter note, I exercised my right to free expression today. I voted for president.
JEFF	And so did I.
SCOTT	Me, too!
MAUREEN	Me, too. Does that mean we're old folks?
JEFF	If it does, may we live to be a hundred!
SCOTT	There were a lot of young people in the line to vote today. And some of the workers didn't look much older than college age, either.
INA	Some people say it's our duty to vote. I call it a privilege. And I'm glad I voted.
MAUREEN	And here we sit waiting for the results. I wonder who will be our next president?
JEFF	We'll know who he is the minute the band strikes up "Hail to the Chief."
MAUREEN	Does anybody know the words to that song?
INA	It has words?
SCOTT	*(picks up a magazine)*
	Yep. I just happened to see them in this magazine today. Would you like to hear them?

JEFF   Sure, but only if you don't try singing them with-
              out music.

SCOTT   Oh, my voice isn't so bad. Here they are:

              Hail to the Chief we have chosen for the nation,
              Hail to the Chief! We salute him, one and all.
              Hail to the Chief, as we pledge cooperation
              In proud fulfillment of a great, noble call.

MAUREEN   I'm glad you found that, Scott. I never heard it
              before.

SCOTT   There's another verse. Wanna hear it?

INA   *(laughs)*

              Do we have a choice? No, seriously, I'd like to
              hear it.

SCOTT   OK, here goes.

              Yours is the aim to make this grand country grander,
              This you will do, that's our strong, firm belief.
              Hail to the one we selected as commander,
              Hail to the President! Hail to the Chief!

JEFF   *(holds up a hand for silence)*

              Shhh. They're playing it now. I think they have a
              winner!

ALL   Yeah!

Section 3

Seasonal and Holidays

April Fool's Joke

Characters: Lavonne
                 Don
                 Howard
                 Pam

Setting: The breakfast room at Brookfield Manor

Props: 4 cups

· ·

LAVONNE   *(sips coffee)*

                 Well, I've already been caught in an April Fool's
                 trick and it's not even noon yet.

DON   What happened?

LAVONNE   Oh, some wise guy must have been dialing numbers
                 at random and he got mine. Told me I had just won
                 the State Lottery.

DON   Did you believe him?

LAVONNE   He caught me off guard because I had actually
                 bought a ticket at the grocery store. Then it
                 occurred to me that he wouldn't know my name,
                 since tickets only have numbers on them. So I hung
                 up on him.

HOWARD   Good for you. But that reminds me of when I was a
                 kid. My friends and I called a really poor woman
                 and played a terrible April Fool's trick on her.

PAM   What did you do?

HOWARD   We took it further than Lavonne's caller did. We
                 said we were from a radio station and if she could
                 answer a question, she'd win a refrigerator. She
                 answered the question and we told her she'd won.

PAM   That's not very nice. Did you admit it was a trick?

HOWARD   No, we played along with her and said it would be delivered to her house. She was so happy she cried. We hung up without telling her the truth.

LAVONNE Poor woman. Tricks like that are mean.

DON   Yeah, but he was just a kid when he did it. He meant no harm.

PAM   Once, my girlfriends and I hung a sign on back of our minister's car. It said "I pick up female sinners." He drove around town all day before he found it there.

HOWARD   Did you get caught?

PAM   No, but I heard his wife was really mad. And the sermon the next Sunday was on the evil of "bearing false witness against your neighbor."

DON   We used to tell people their shoelaces were untied. Or their zippers were open.

HOWARD   My buddy and I turned a chicken loose in the main hall at school. Then everybody stood around scaring it when the janitor was trying to catch it.

DON   *(laughs)*

             My friends and I took the seats out of our band leader's car and put them on the flat roof of the auditorium. Then we stuffed a band uniform, put a false face on it and set it on the seat with a bass drum.

PAM   Didn't anybody see you doing that?

DON   I guess not. We didn't get in trouble.

PAM   Once, I bumped against my English teacher and taped a long strip of toilet paper onto the back of her skirt just as she went on stage for an assembly. Everybody shrieked with laughter.

HOWARD   What about you Lavonne, didn't you ever do any bad April Fool's tricks?

LAVONNE   Of course not! I don't believe in tricks. You guys should be ashamed!

HOWARD   Oh, so we have Little Miss Goody Two Shoes with us, do we?

LAVONNE   *(leans close to Howard)*

                    Howard, what is that on your chin? Is it egg yolk?

HOWARD   You're not getting me on that old trick, Lavonne!

LAVONNE   *(smiles sweetly)*

                    OK. So don't brush it off. Walk around like that!

HOWARD   You know I have to check my chin, don't you?

                    (brushes his chin)

LAVONNE   *(points)*

                    A little more to the right.

                    (points again)

                    No, more to the left.

HOWARD   *(brushes again)*

LAVONNE   *(smiles sweetly)*

                    Looks like Little Miss Goody Two Shoes Got'cha!

ALL   *(laughs)*

                    April Fool!

Biggest Little Show on Earth

Characters: Barker
             Harry
             June

Setting: The entrance to the carnival

Props: None

. . . .

BARKER   *(dramatically)*

Step right up Ladies and Gentlemen, Children of
All Ages! Step right this way to the Biggest Little Show On Earth!

HARRY   I like coming to the carnival! There's so much to
see.

JUNE   Me too! I especially like the wild animals and the
lion tamers.

BARKER   *(grandly gestures toward the left)*

In the tent to my left you will see Saleem, The
Scintillating Sword Swallower...the man with the
Exceptional Esophagus.

JUNE   Oh, the Sword Swallower! Have you ever seen anybody do that? It's unbelievable!

BARKER   One slip, just a fraction of an inch, and the
sword could slice through Saleem's throat like a
needle through a noodle!

HARRY   That sounds pretty dangerous to me.

BARKER   *(waves hand)*

Get your tickets now. The Marvelous Magic Show is
about to begin in the tent to my right.

JUNE Magic shows are great fun.

BARKER Or if your favorite feature is the future, the great mystic, Madame Moira LaPalma will read that road for you.

JUNE The mystic would be fun. I wonder what my future holds. Riches? Fame?

HARRY *(shakes head)*

Or perhaps just a normal life?

BARKER *(points behind himself)*

Go through the turnstile behind this very stage and you will witness even more Incredible Deeds of Daring. The Balancing Baldini Family will dazzle you on the high wire.

JUNE Oh, the high wire act! It's unbelievable what they can do on a thin wire.

BARKER Does anybody here not love a lithe and lovely lady? Come right on in and thrill to the limber Lady Letisha as she performs amazing acrobatics on the bare back of a galloping gelding.

HARRY Lady Letisha! I've heard of her. She's supposed to be really good.

BARKER *(points up)*

And high above the big top, your heart will stop at the aerial antics of The Flying Zoltan! He's as much at ease on the flying trapeze as your granny is resting in her rocking chair.

JUNE That's it! We're going in there. I want to see the Flying Zoltan!

HARRY *(slaps forehead)*

I should have known you'd go for that big lug!

(sings and motions everybody to join in)

ALL

For once I was happy, But now I'm forlorn.
Just like an old coat that is tattered and torn.
Left in this wide world to fret and to mourn.
Betrayed by a maid in her teens.

Now this girl that I loved, she was handsome.
And I tried all I knew, her to please.
But I never could please her one-quarter so well
As the man on the flying trapeze.

Oh! He floats through the air with the greatest of ease
This daring young man on the flying trapeze
His movements are graceful, All the girls he does please
And my love he has purloined away.

Father's Day

Characters: Bob
             Vickie

Setting: On the front porch of Shady Acres Senior Center

Props: None

....

VICKIE   Do you have any plans for today, Bob?

BOB   Actually, yes. It's Father's Day, so my son is
             picking me up and taking me to his house for
             dinner.

VICKIE   That sounds nice. I'm going to my daughter's house
             to celebrate with her and her husband and the
             kids. She said her sons are making a party for
             their dad.

BOB   Are the sons doing the cooking?

VICKIE   Yes. They're learning even though they're still
             pretty young. My daughter has taught them how to
             make some simple things.

BOB   That's nice. What can they cook?

VICKIE   Oh, grilled cheese and a can of soup. And she
             helped them bake a cake and frost it.

BOB   That should be fun. I'll bet the kids will enjoy
             showing off their skills.

VICKIE   Probably. Their mom believes boys need to know the
             basics for taking care of themselves. She says
             they'll need to know when they're in college, or
             when they get jobs.

BOB   Good idea. If they can cook, they won't have to
             eat everything at fast food places.

VICKIE	It's a chance for them to do something nice for their father, too.
	(sighs)
	You know, this day always makes me think of my own dad. We were so close.
BOB	Then you must have good memories of him.
VICKIE	I do. When I was a little girl I had to reach up to hold his hand. I loved it when he'd put me on his shoulders and prance like a pony.
BOB	Little girls have a special way of winning their fathers' affections.
VICKIE	And I took advantage of that to get my own way. He let me get by with murder, but he was also very protective of me. He practically interviewed anybody I went out with.
BOB	What did the boys think of that?
VICKIE	Oh, I don't think they really minded. Later on, my husband was the same way with my daughter. It just shows how much they care.
BOB	Well, I only had a son, but I can imagine.
VICKIE	Were you close with your father, Bob?
BOB	Never knew him. He left Mom and my brother and me when I was too young to remember him.
VICKIE	Oh, no!
BOB	It's OK because it all worked out. Mom remarried when I was seven.
VICKIE	That's nice.
BOB	Yeah, but when I look back, it's a wonder we didn't scare him away. Neither of us wanted to share Mom, and we were really brats. A lot of men would have turned on their heels and run...fast.

VICKIE   What did you do?

BOB   Every thing we could think of. When he came over, we'd fight and yell and spill things just to be obnoxious. Every time he sat down, I'd pretend to trip over his feet.

VICKIE   How did he handle the bad manners?

BOB   *(laughs)*

               Firmly. I used to think he married Mom just so he could say, "I'm head of this house now. And you will answer to me!" And we did.

VICKIE   Amazing. Your mother was a lucky woman.

BOB   We all were. Dad...he made us call him Dad right from the first day...Dad taught us how to fix our bikes, and later our cars. We did things together. We fished and camped and went on vacations. He was a great guy.

VICKIE   It sounds like he was.

BOB   Once, on Halloween, my brother and I dumped the garbage cans out on the school lawn. We got caught and the principal called my folks.

VICKIE   Oh, my. What did he do?

BOB   Well, Dad told the principal to do what he had to do and he'd understand.

VICKIE   You mean he'd approve of your getting reported to the police?

BOB   Well, he went on to suggest they make a deal. If the principal would drop charges, Dad would see that we cleaned up the mess. Plus, he'd make us work a month with the janitorial staff keeping the grounds clean...for free.

VICKIE   Wow, he was tough. Do you ever wonder what your real father might have been like, Bob?

BOB   I know what he was like, Vickie. That's why Dad is my "real father." Oh, there's my son. I've got to go.

VICKIE   OK, Bob. Happy Father's Day.

BOB   You too, Vickie.

Favorite Season

Characters: Claire
              Al
              Pauline
              Greg

Setting: Near a bay window at the senior center

Props: None

. . . .

AL   Have you noticed how the view is always changing
              at this window?

CLAIRE   *(grumpily)*

              That same house is still across the street. To the
              left of it is another house. And to the right is
              another one that's always been there.

AL   That's not all that I see.

CLAIRE   Oh, sure. The houses have front yards. And a few
              trees.

AL   And snow on the ground?

CLAIRE   Of course not. It's summer.

AL   And the sun is too bright?

CLAIRE   It's raining, and I'm getting tired of this con-
              versation.

PAULINE   I think I know what you're saying, Al. The view
              does change.

GREG   *(teasingly)*

              So, we've got two poets in our midst, have we?
              I'll play along. What difference do you see be-
              tween today and yesterday, Pauline?

PAULINE   Well, yesterday the driveway was white concrete. Today it's a silver river.

CLAIRE   Give me strength!

GREG   *(looks out)*

She's right, Al. The river may not be as deep as the Mississippi. But it's a river all right. It has sticks and leaves floating toward the street.

PAULINE   And you can even see the current from here.

AL   What do you think, Claire?

CLAIRE   I think the water is flowing down to the street like it always does when it rains.

AL   Like a...what?

CLAIRE   Stop it, Al.

(pauses)

Well, it's certainly not a very big river!

PAULINE   Hey, this is kind of fun. Those cars going by make waves like a motorboat.

AL   Look at the trees, too. They're hanging lower than yesterday. And you can see which way the wind is blowing.

CLAIRE   That's enough, you guys. It's raining, that's all.

GREG   OK. But first, without looking at it, tell me what color that brick house is directly across the street.

CLAIRE   It's red, Greg. Red brick.

GREG   Check again, Claire. It's brown.

CLAIRE   That's because it's wet.

AL   Summer is nice, but winter is still my favorite season.

CLAIRE   Winter is cold, Al. It's nobody's favorite season.

GREG   Why do you like winter, Al?

AL   I like looking at all the tracks in the snow.
                Tracks from the squirrels, the dogs, cats, people,
                cars.

PAULINE   My husband always liked the fall colors. We'd al-
                ways go up in the woods in the fall to see the
                leaves change.

CLAIRE   I'd have to say that spring is my favorite season.

PAULINE   Why, Claire?

CLAIRE   Everything seems to wake up in the spring.

                (pauses, then laughs)

                It's sort of like the winter's bad mood gets better.

AL   *(grins)*

                Sort of like people, eh, Claire?

CLAIRE   *(smiles and nods sheepishly)*

                Yeah, sort of like people.

For Auld Lang Syne

Note to Activity Director: Before this skit is performed, photocopy the lyrics (page 48) and pass them out to all participants.

Characters: Phil
               Irene
               Clarence
               Helen

Setting: The Ballroom of the Chez Ami Hotel on New Year's Eve

Props: Four glasses

• •

PHIL   It's getting so loud in here I can barely hear you.

CLARENCE   That's because it's nearly midnight.

IRENE   Just three more minutes 'til twelve o'clock!

CLARENCE   Another new year is almost here.

HELEN   Where'd the old year go?

PHIL   *(holds up glass)*

                 Well, before it gets too loud, I want to be the first to say Happy New Year to all of you!

                 (they all click glasses)

ALL   Hear, hear!

IRENE   I hope we celebrate a lot more new years together!

CLARENCE   I'll second that. This has been a great year for Helen and me. We took a nice vacation. We're both feeling good. I love New Year's Eve.

HELEN   And I love a party. We don't even know most of these people here and they're all acting like family.

PHIL   I like it when people are all friendly with each
                other.

IRENE   We should celebrate more than once a year. What
                other time do I get to dance right through the
                toes of my nylons?

                (wiggles a foot)

CLARENCE   *(looks up)*

                And what other time of year do they drop a thousand
                balloons down from the ceiling?

HELEN   When else does the band play with this much enthu-
                siasm?

PHIL   *(pats stomach)*

                And everybody eats too much because their resolu-
                tions go into effect at midnight?

IRENE   And everybody drinks a little too much champagne?

CLARENCE   Look, they have a picture of the ball drop in Times
                Square on the big screen. We can watch them count
                down, too.

HELEN   *(laughs)*

                Well, I wish they were flashing a picture of us on a
                screen in Times Square! Wouldn't that be something!

PHIL   One more minute to go!

IRENE   OK. Does everybody know all four stanzas of Auld
                Lang Syne?

CLARENCE   I know the first one. Then I fake it.

HELEN   So do I. Who could hear the real words anyway?

PHIL   I've heard the words. And they don't make sense to
                me.

HELEN   It doesn't matter what the words are. I'll cry. I
                always cry.

PHIL   Helen, you cry over everything...whether it's good
               news or bad news.

HELEN   That's why I don't wear mascara.

CLARENCE   *(laughs)*

               Just look around the room...there will be lots of
               people crying.

IRENE   Don't worry. I always have a tissue.

PHIL   The band leader has his baton up. They're about to
               start the count.

HELEN   And they're showing the ball on the big screen.

CLARENCE   Get ready.

PHIL   OK. Here goes. Ten. Nine.

ALL   Eight. Seven. Six. Five. Four. Three. Two. One.
               Happy New Year!

(Phil gestures for everybody in the room to sing along.)

ALL   *Should auld acquaintance be forgot, And never brought to mind?*
          Should auld acquaintance be forgot, And days of Auld Lang Syne?

          (Chorus) For Auld Lang Syne, my dear, For Auld Lang Syne.
          We'll take a cup of kindness yet, For Auld Lang Syne.

          We twa hae run aboot the braes, And pu'd the gowans fine.
          We've wander'd many a weary foot, Sin Auld Lang Syne.
          (repeat chorus)

          We twa ha'e sported i' the burn, Frae marnin' sun till dine.
          But seas between us braid ha'e roared, Sin Auld Lang Syne.
          (repeat chorus)

          And here's a hand my trusty frien', And gie a hand o' thine.
          We'll tak' a cup of kindness yet, For Auld Lang Syne.
          (repeat chorus)

(Both women wipe away a tear. The men raise their glasses and clink them.)

ALL   Happy New Year!

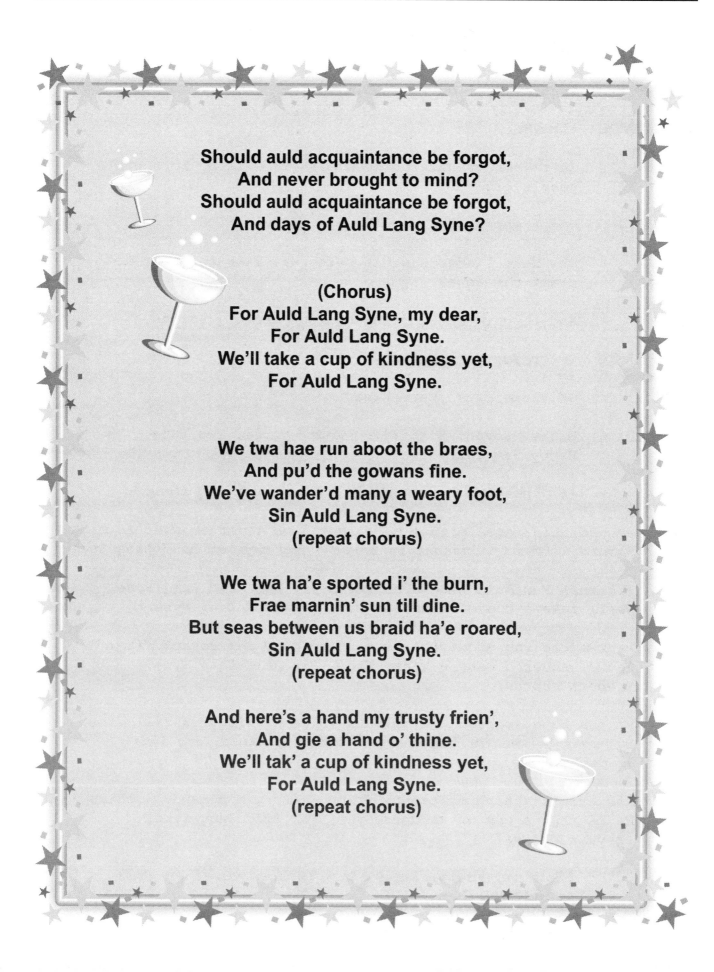

Should auld acquaintance be forgot,
And never brought to mind?
Should auld acquaintance be forgot,
And days of Auld Lang Syne?

(Chorus)
For Auld Lang Syne, my dear,
For Auld Lang Syne.
We'll take a cup of kindness yet,
For Auld Lang Syne.

We twa hae run aboot the braes,
And pu'd the gowans fine.
We've wander'd many a weary foot,
Sin Auld Lang Syne.
(repeat chorus)

We twa ha'e sported i' the burn,
Frae marnin' sun till dine.
But seas between us braid ha'e roared,
Sin Auld Lang Syne.
(repeat chorus)

And here's a hand my trusty frien',
And gie a hand o' thine.
We'll tak' a cup of kindness yet,
For Auld Lang Syne.
(repeat chorus)

Holiday Cards (For Any Holiday)

Note to Activity Director: Once this skit is performed, participants may wish to make their own greeting cards.

Characters: Grandma Olive
              Kimberly, her young granddaughter

Setting: A couch in the social room of Seaside Senior Home

Props: A box of supplies with two large white papers, bits of
              colored paper, glue pen, felt tip pens

. . . .

KIMBERLY   Hi, Grandma. Mamma dropped me off and she'll be
               here as soon as she stops by the drug store.

GRANDMA   Hi, Sweetie. It's so nice to see you. What have
               you got there?

KIMBERLY   Well, I was going to get you a card, then decided
               it would be more fun to bring my supplies and we
               can each make one.

GRANDMA   What a nice idea!

KIMBERLY   *(sits down beside Grandma and offers box of supplies)*

               Here, you take a paper and I'll keep one. Now, you
               fold yours in the middle, then again in the middle.

               (both fold their papers)

               See. Now we each have a card to work on.

GRANDMA   OK. It's starting to look like a card. Now what?

KIMBERLY   Take some of these colored papers and make yourself
               a design. A flower, tree, house, whatever you like.

GRANDMA   *(glues on some designs)*

               Oh, this is fun. Look at my picture.

KIMBERLY   That's pretty, Grandma. Look at mine!

            (shows her card)

            Now, when we're done with the front, open it up
            and we'll make a verse inside.

GRANDMA   I know what mine is going to say.

KIMBERLY   Me too. But don't tell until we're done.

            (both write for a moment)

GRANDMA   Mine is done. Would you like to see it?

KIMBERLY   Mine's done, too. Show me yours first.

GRANDMA   *(shows her card)*

            See, the front is a flower.

            (opens it)

            And inside it says: "To my granddaughter: Just
            like a flower, you bring me all the freshness and
            beauty of springtime. Love, Grandma."

KIMBERLY   *(hugs her grandmother)*

            Thanks, Grandma. I'll put this on my dresser.

GRANDMA   OK. Now show me your card.

KIMBERLY   *(shows the front)*

            See, the front has a picture of an evergreen tree.

            (opens it)

            And inside it says: "Dear Grandma, This tree
            reminds me of your strength. And like you, it is
            ever green. Love, Kimberly"

GRANDMA   *(takes the card)*

            This is going on my dresser. No, no it's not. This
            one is going on my door! I want everybody to see it.

It Came Upon A Midnight Clear

Characters: Joseph
                Shoshana

Setting: The doorway of an inn in Bethlehem

Prop: Cup of water

. . . .

JOSEPH   *(knocks on door)*

Hello! Is anybody here?

SHOSHANA Who is it?

JOSEPH   My name is Joseph, madam. My wife and I need lodging for the night.

SHOSHANA I'm very sorry, sir. The inn is closed. We have no more rooms to let.

JOSEPH   Please don't send me away. My wife is with child. She's weary from our journey and she cannot go on.

SHOSHANA Sir, I wish I could help. But the roads are crowded with travelers, and our rooms have been filled all week. There is no room in this inn for even one more person, certainly not room for two!

JOSEPH   Madam, we would take any lodging you could give us. Anything! Look at Mary over there. She is so tired she can barely sit upright on our donkey.

SHOSHANA Oh, the poor dear is so large with child! Why are you traveling? She should be at home.

JOSEPH   That's true. But we are obeying the decree of Caesar Augustus. We came here to Bethlehem, the City of David, to pay our taxes.

SHOSHANA There must be a better way to collect taxes than to force a mother-to-be out on the highway on a donkey.

JOSEPH   Please, madam. I know if you will just give Mary a place to sleep for tonight, that God will bless you.

SHOSHANA   I don't have a place. But, get her down and bring her over here. She can rest on a chair for a while.

JOSEPH   Thank you, madam.

SHOSHANA   She can only rest a little while. Then you'll have to find another place to stay.

JOSEPH   I know you have a kind heart.

SHOSHANA   That's true, I do. It pains me to send this woman out on the road in her condition.

JOSEPH   There must be a corner or a hallway where she could stay.

SHOSHANA   *(presses her hands against her temples)*

It's against my better judgment, but there is a place where she can sleep.

JOSEPH   Oh, thank you! I'll go get her.

SHOSHANA   First, let me make one thing clear. It's not a room with a bed. It's just a manger...with cattle in it. But it will give her a roof over her head. And I will have my husband spread fresh hay down to make a bed for her.

JOSEPH   Thank you! We're so grateful.

SHOSHANA   *(hands him a cup)*

Here, give her some cool water, then bring her here. I can't offer you much, but you're welcome to what I have.

JOSEPH   Madam, I can't thank you enough. And you cannot possibly know what a blessing your kindness is.

(pauses, and looks to the side)

Mary, we have found a place for you to rest.

(walks offstage)

SHOSHANA *(looks up)*

> Why, look! The clouds have blown away. And the
> stars are shining. It's looks like it's going to
> be a nice night after all.

> *(gestures for everyone to join in the singing)*

ALL
> *It came upon a midnight clear*
> *That glorious song of old*
> *The angels bending near the earth*
> *To touch their harps of gold.*
> *Peace on the earth, good will to men*
> *From Heaven's all gracious King*
> *The world in solemn stillness lay*
> *To hear the angels sing.*

Jingle All The Way

Characters: Chris (a woman or a man)
              Pat (a woman or a man)

Setting: A window at Willow Grove Senior Home

Props: None

· ·

CHRIS   Hello, Pat. Beautiful morning, isn't it?

PAT   Hi Chris. It sure is.

CHRIS   We must have had two feet of snow last night.

PAT   At least! It's pretty when it's fresh.

CHRIS   Like a postcard.

PAT   Speaking of cards, I finished writing all my holiday cards last night. It's a big job.

CHRIS   You're ahead of me. I haven't even bought mine yet. I'm going out later to buy some Christmas cards for my Christian friends and some Hanukkah cards for my Jewish friends.

PAT   Did you do your holiday shopping yet?

CHRIS   Not yet. But I'm going to try to get to it today. How about you?

PAT   No, I haven't gotten to that yet. But I have started phoning some of the people I haven't seen for a while. I do that once a year.

CHRIS   I started phoning my old friends, too. In fact, two of them are coming to see me later today.

PAT   I like this time of year. It seems like we always take a little more time getting in touch with people we know.

CHRIS   And reminiscing.

(leans toward window)

That snow reminds me of so many good times. Why don't we put on our coats and boots and go out there on the porch for a while?

PAT   Sounds good to me. I might even toss a snowball or two at you.

CHRIS   Well, you'd better be quick. They didn't used to call me "Deadeye Chris" for nothing.

PAT   Come on, let's get those coats.

(both begin singing softly)

PAT/CHRIS *Dashing through the snow,*
In a one-horse open sleigh,
O'er the fields we go,
Laughing all the way.

(motions for others to join them)

ALL   *Bells on bob-tails ring,*
Making spirits bright,
What fun it is to ride and sing,
a sleighing song tonight.

(louder)

Jingle Bells, Jingle Bells,
Jingle all the way.
Oh, what fun it is to ride
in a one-horse open sleigh.
Jingle Bells, Jingle Bells,
Jingle all the way.
Oh, what fun it is to ride
in a one-horse open sleigh.

(repeat)

National Hugging Day

(Observed January 21st)

Characters: Charlotte
              Annette
              George
              Owen

Setting: The social room at Snug Haven Senior Residence

Prop: Piece of paper

. . . .

CHARLOTTE *(points to paper)*

Look. The social calendar says today is National Hugging Day.

ANNETTE   That's nice. But I'm a little selective about whom I want to hug.

GEORGE   Oh, lighten up, Annette. I'll bet before this day is over you'll give somebody or something a hug.

ANNETTE   Ha. Don't count on it, George.

OWEN   I read an article that said people who are huggers live longer than people who aren't.

CHARLOTTE *(smiles and nods)*

That makes sense to me, since I hug everyone from my grandchildren to the girl who does my nails. Annette, I'll bet you hug your visitors when they come over.

ANNETTE   I didn't say I never hug anybody. I just said I'm selective.

GEORGE   So am I. In fact, I was thinking of giving a hugging audition. I'll give everybody a chance to try out, and when it's over, I'll make my selection and decide who gets seconds.

OWEN   George, if National Hugging day were every day of the year, you'd want 365 days of auditions.

CHARLOTTE Except on leap year, then he'd want that extra day.

ANNETTE Well, to each his own. Some people pass out their hugs as easily as a politician shakes hands. Then the hugs don't mean anything.

GEORGE   A hug is similar to a handshake. It's just a handshake with more enthusiasm.

OWEN   *(grins)*

I hugged a horse this morning.

CHARLOTTE Oh, stop it, Owen! You hugged a horse?!

OWEN   Yep. I took my walk like always, and I saw this old red horse tied up to a tree in the park. I petted his neck, and he rolled his head around in my hand. So I gave him a hug.

CHARLOTTE Aw, that's sweet.

ANNETTE I knew a woman once who would have hugged the tree, not the horse.

OWEN   Oh, sure. Like she hugged trees!

ANNETTE She did. If a tree was about to get cut down, her group would link arms around it to stop the woodcutters.

GEORGE   Trees aren't half as much fun as the audition I had in mind.

ANNETTE I used to work with this guy, Donald, who came to the office and patted the men on the shoulder and hugged the ladies.

CHARLOTTE Did you mind that?

ANNETTE I usually kept out of his way. Then one day the boss sent a memo saying all touching had to stop. Something about sexual harassment in the workplace.

GEORGE   Mind if I asked who it was that complained, Annette?

ANNETTE   No, it wasn't me, George, even though I was never
                  approved of it. In fact, I'll admit that the of-
                  fice wasn't as warm after that.

OWEN   People do have to be careful about seeming too
                  friendly. Some people resent it and others feel
                  threatened by too much closeness.

CHARLOTTE   Oh, I think it's quite clear when somebody gives a
                  back-pat or a hug in friendliness, and when it's
                  inappropriate.

GEORGE   So do I. Even a dog makes it clear. When he rubs
                  his nose on your hand, you know he's glad to see
                  you and he's not going to bite you.

CHARLOTTE   Last week when I wasn't feeling well, the night
                  nurse came and gave me my medicine. That's all she
                  really had to do, but you know what? When she left
                  she gave me a hug. Then I felt better.

OWEN   That's probably why that study says huggers live
                  longer. It's the warm feeling people get from hugs.

ANNETTE   I'll admit I did hug Margaret out at the reception
                  desk today. She went out of her way to help me
                  open my mailbox, so I sort of hugged her in appre-
                  ciation.

GEORGE   See! I was right, wasn't I?

ANNETTE   Don't be so smug, George. That just proved how
                  selective I am. My hugs have meaning.

CHARLOTTE   So does a boa constrictor's.

OWEN   *(laughs)*

                  Now, that might mess up the study a little.

We Wish You Our Very Best

Characters: Ben
              Grace
              Terry

Setting: The living room of The Elms Senior Residence

Props: None

. . . .

BEN   Hi, Grace. You're all dressed up. Have you been to church?

GRACE   Yes. The service was really special today.

TERRY   Really? What was good about it?

GRACE   The sermon was entitled "Give your *PRESENCE,* not your *PRESENTS,* this holiday season."

TERRY   Presence, not presents? What, exactly, does that mean?

GRACE   Well, it had a lot to do with the fact that the real message of the season, for both Christians and Jews, is getting lost in materialism today.

BEN   You can say that again! Seems like the commercials for holiday merchandise start earlier every year.

TERRY   They really do. And the things they advertise get bigger and more expensive all the time.

GRACE   Being aware of that was only part of the sermon. We also need to guard against letting ourselves think holidays are just days for gifts.

BEN   Good idea. Did you get any suggestions for making changes?

GRACE   Actually, yes. We can try to think of the word "presence" every time we want to give a present to someone.

TERRY   I'm not sure I understand.

GRACE   OK. Suppose you're sending a holiday card to some-
                 one you haven't seen for a while. Instead of just
                 signing your name, put your presence, or yourself,
                 into the card. Write a note inside it. That shows
                 you care.

BEN   I like getting more than just a name on my cards.
                 A note is sort of like getting a visit.

GRACE   Right! Sometimes a few words will cheer a lonely
                 person.

TERRY   Does that mean we're not supposed to give gifts
                 any more?

GRACE   Oh, no, not at all! Again, *PRESENCE*—not *PRESENTS*—
                 means giving something from your heart. For in-
                 stance, if a person loves to embroider, giving
                 nice thread would be more personal than perfume.

TERRY   I see. Making the gift personal is putting my
                 presence into it.

BEN   Right. That would show you know what she enjoys.

GRACE   Exactly. How about the people here in our hospital
                 section? You know how we always take up a collec-
                 tion to buy each of them a little gift?

TERRY   Sure. That's a tradition here.

GRACE   Well, the presents are just fine. I'm sure they
                 enjoy getting something.

BEN   OK, I sense the word "presence" is about to come.

GRACE   Yes, it is. Why don't we all take those gifts and
                 give them to the patients personally? We could
                 plan to sit with them a while and just chat.

TERRY   They'd enjoy that. And you know something? I think
                 I would, too.

BEN   But some of them are sick. They wouldn't have a
                 lot to say to us.

GRACE　　　We can do the talking, or just be there for a few minutes.

BEN　　　What should we talk about?

GRACE　　　We would just be ourselves and say what is in our hearts.

BEN　　　Such as?

TERRY　　　We could ask them about their children. Or what their jobs they did when they worked. Or just chat about the food.

GRACE　　　Or maybe we could talk about good times that we've known, and ask about their favorite memories.

BEN　　　Let's see what the others think about sharing their presence.

GRACE　　　And after we've visited, we could sing a holiday song or two.

TERRY　　　A cheerful one.

GRACE　　　How about "We Wish You a Merry Christmas!" for our Christian friends?

BEN　　　Good idea. And how about "Hava Nagila" for our Jewish friends?

TERRY　　　OK. Let's practice. And put our presence in it.

(gestures for everybody to sing)

ALL　　　*We wish you a Merry Christmas,*
We wish you a Merry Christmas,
We wish you a Merry Christmas,
and a Happy New Year.

Good tidings to you,
And all of your kin,
Good tidings for Christmas,
and a Happy New Year.

(please turn page for "Hava Nagila")

Hava Nagila, Hava Nagila,
Hava Nagila, Va nis m' Chayh.
Hava Nagila, Hava Nigila,
Hava Nagila, Vay nis m' Chayh.
Hava Nagila, Vay nis m' Chayh.
Hava Nigila, Vay nis m' Chayh.
U- Ru, U-Ru A-Chim,
U-Ru A-Chim, B'Lev Sa-me-ach,
U-Ru A-Chim, B'Lev Sa-me-ach,
U-Ru A-Chim, B'Lev Sa-me-ach,
U-Ru A—Chim, B'Lev Sa-me-ach.

Section 4

Just for Fun

Bonnie, Come Back

Characters: Betty
             Goldie
             Segal

Setting: Betty and Goldie at the front door of Segal's house

Prop: A large paper bag or cake carrier

. . . .

BETTY   Nobody answered. I wonder if anybody is home. Should I ring again?

GOLDIE   I hear footsteps.

               (Segal appears)

               Hello, Segal.

SEGAL   Hello, Betty. Hello, Goldie.

BETTY   Hi, Segal. We heard Bonnie is sick so we brought her a cake.

SEGAL   *(sadly)*

               No, Bonnie isn't sick. Not unless she happens to be homesick.

GOLDIE   Aw, does she still miss Scotland after all these years?

SEGAL   No, I mean she's gone. She's not here at home.

BETTY   Bonnie's not here?

SEGAL   She's not here. She left me.

GOLDIE   She left you?

SEGAL   She left me. She split. She flew the coop.

BETTY   She flew...?

SEGAL   *(nods)*

Yes. She's vamoosed. Cut out. Vanished. Disappeared.

GOLDIE   Oh, don't worry, Segal. She's just lonely for Scotland. She'll be back.

SEGAL   No, she's gone this time. For good.

BETTY   Bonnie just misses her old stomping grounds. That's all. I know she'll be back.

GOLDIE   I hope so. But in the meantime, if there's anything at all that we can do...

SEGAL   There is. Find her and tell her to come home.

GOLDIE   But where would we look? What if she really went back to Scotland?

SEGAL   Call her mother. Write to her sister. I'll buy your tickets if you have to go to Scotland to get her. But somehow, bring her back.

              (starts singing, motions everyone to join in)

ALL   *My Bonnie lies over the ocean.*
My Bonnie lies over the sea.
My Bonnie lies over the ocean.
Oh, bring back my Bonnie to me.

Bring back, bring back,
Oh, Bring back my Bonnie to me. To me.
Bring back, bring back,
Oh, Bring back my Bonnie to me.

(repeat)

Hinkey Dinkey Make Some Sense

Characters: Sadie
              Jackie
              Arnie

Setting: The sun room

Props: None

. . . .

SADIE   Gee, it seems awfully quiet in here today. Don't
               they usually have some music playing?

JACKIE   There was music when I came in but I turned it off.

ARNIE   Why'd you turn it off, Jackie? Did you just prefer
               quiet?

JACKIE   No, but the songs they were playing didn't make
               any sense. The words were too silly to understand.

SADIE   Some songs are pretty silly. And not just the new
               songs, either.

ARNIE   One of my all time favorite singers is Bob Dylan,
               and frankly, I never did understand a word he said.
               He sounds like he has a mouth full of marbles.

SADIE   I guess somebody must understand him because he
               has sold a whole lot of records.

JACKIE   Why don't they play more Grand Opera on radio?
               Opera music is so moving. And the voices are so
               beautiful.

ARNIE   Most opera is in Italian, Jackie. And the only
               Italian word I understand is "pizza."

SADIE   You wanna understand songs? Does anybody here re-
               member "Mairzy Doats"?

ARNIE   "...and do-zy doats and lid-dle lam-zy div-ey."
               Now, isn't that catchy?

SADIE   They are really saying "mares eat oats and does eat oats and little lambs eat ivy, a kid'll eat ivy, too, wouldn't you?" but it doesn't really make sense until you see it written out.

JACKIE   Next you'll tell us that you liked "Hut Sut Rawl-son on the rill-er-ah and a braw-la, braw-la soo-it."

ARNIE   Sure, I liked that one. It got my foot to tapping. So did "Chick-er-y chick, cha-la, cha-la."

SADIE   I still love all the old "Doo Wop" songs. They have a great beat. I have a whole collection that I play when I'm in the mood.

JACKIE   What ever happened to the standards? Where did Irving Berlin go? And Rodgers and Hammerstein?

SADIE   Do you mean the old show tunes? They're still around. They're classics.

JACKIE   That's what I want to hear. Opera and the classics.

ARNIE   *(grins mischievously)*

You wanna hear a classic? I've got one for you. Will you sing along?

JACKIE   *(shrugs)*

I guess so.

ARNIE   Here goes, but you have to sing it with me.

ALL   The Mademoiselle from Armentieres, Parlez Vous.
The Mademoiselle from Armentieres, Parlez Vous.
The Mademoiselle from Armentieres,
She hadn't been kissed for a hundred years.
Hinkey-Dinkey Parlez Vous.

Two German officers crossed the Rhine, Parlez Vous.
Two German officers crossed the Rhine, Parlez Vous.
Two German officers crossed the Rhine
To kiss the women and drink the wine.
Hinkey-Dinkey Parlez Vous.

JACKIE   Enough of the classics! Now, if you don't mind, we'll just leave the radio off for a while. OK?

Just Ask Sara

Characters: Sara Bellum, Host
              Alison
              Thelma
              Randall
              Wilson
              Rich
              Dawn
              Travis

Setting: A phone-in radio show, "The Sara Bellum Show"

Prop: Phone

. . . .

SARA   *(brightly)*

              Hello. This is "The Sara Bellum Show." Sara speaking. We're on the air. What is your question?

ALISON   Oh, hello Sara. My name is Alison and I'm worried about something.

SARA   Thanks for calling, Alison. What's your problem?

ALISON   Well, I think my boyfriend is losing interest in me and I don't know what to do about it.

SARA   What makes you think he's losing interest in you?

ALISON   Every time he sits down next to me, he dozes off and mumbles other women's names in his sleep.

SARA   Oh, sweetie, not to worry. You can buy some little foam rubber earplugs at any drug store. Use them and you won't hear a thing.

SARA   *(puts phone to ear)*

              It's "The Sara Bellum Show." Tell me your problem.

THELMA   Hello, Sara. This is Thelma. I'm in a real quandary.

SARA	Thelma, honey, just ask Sara. That's what I'm here for.
THELMA	Yesterday I got this letter from an old high school sweetheart. He was my first love.
SARA	Well, that's real nice, Thelma. Everybody needs to be loved. There's nothing wrong with that.
THELMA	But he said he still has feelings for me.
SARA	What more could a girl ask?
THELMA	You don't understand. I'm married. Should I show the letter to my husband?
SARA	Was it addressed to him?
THELMA	No.
SARA	Well, it's against the law for people to read other people's mail, Thelma. You don't want your husband to get in trouble with the law, do you?
THELMA	Goodness, no.
SARA	Well, you've answered your own question, Thelma. I'm glad I was able to help. Next caller please.
SARA	Hello. This is Sara. Go ahead.
RICH	How ya' doin' Sara? This is Rich and I need some advice.
SARA	Just ask Sara, Rich. That's what I'm here for.
RICH	*(embarrassed)*
	To be honest, Rich isn't my real name.
SARA	That's OK, Rich. I can understand that. What's your question?
RICH	Well, here's my problem. When I filed my income tax report I figured I had $82.00 coming back.
SARA	Wonderful, Rich.

RICH	No, you don't understand. My refund check came but it was for $820.00. Should I contact the IRS and tell them they made a mistake?
SARA	Don't be silly, Rich. Everybody knows it's better to receive than to give.
RICH	But isn't that dishonest?
SARA	You've been paying taxes all your life, haven't you?
RICH	Well, yeah.
SARA	Then just consider this the IRS's way of saying "thank you."
RICH	Oh, if you look at it that way! Thanks Sara. You're a big help.
SARA	Any time, Rich.

(pauses, then answers next line)

Sara Bellum here. Have a problem? Just ask Sara.

RANDALL	Hi there, Sara. Randall here. I need your help with a problem.
SARA	Let's have it, Randall. No problem is too big for Sara to solve.
RANDALL	Well, my daughter's husband lost his job, so the wife and I let them both move in with us until he finds another one.
SARA	You're good people, Randall. There is nothing like helping family to give you a warm glow.
RANDALL	Maybe, but the bum is so comfortable here, he won't even look for a job. I get nervous watching him sit around in front of the TV all day drinking beer.
SARA	That is a problem. You've got to give him exactly two weeks to find a job and move out.
RANDALL	I already did that. He won't go.

SARA	Then, there's only one way to save your nerves. You move out! Next call!
SARA	Hello. You're on the air with "The Sara Bellum Show." Go ahead.
WILSON	Hello, Sara. This is Wilson. My problem is my wife. She's a few years older than I am. It never bothered me until now.
SARA	So why is it suddenly bothering you now?
WILSON	She's slowing down. She never wants to join me in anything I like to do.
SARA	What sort of things do you like to do, Wilson?
WILSON	Oh, the usual. Sky diving, Scuba diving, jet skiing, bungee jumping.
SARA	*(breathlessly)*
	Ohhhh, you sound like a macho man, Wilson. Tell me now, Big Guy, have you told your concerns to your wife?
WILSON	Yes. She won't listen to reason. She won't even talk about it.
SARA	How selfish of her. There's only one way to solve this problem, Wilson.
WILSON	What is it? I'll do anything.
SARA	Simple. Get yourself a younger wife.
	(pauses, then answers next line)
	Hello. It's "The Sara Bellum Show." How can I help you?
DAWN	It's Dawn, Sara. My problem is kinda personal.
SARA	That's OK, honey. Nothing is too personal to share with our listeners. Just ask Sara.
DAWN	OK. Sara, I think I'm in love. No, I'm absolutely certain I'm in love.

SARA   That's wonderful, Dawn. Some people never find love.

DAWN   But you don't understand. I'm in love with Elvis! That black hair, those pouty lips, those swivel hips!

SARA   Mmmmm, this is a dilemma, Dawn. Are you aware that Elvis is...gone?

DAWN   Sure I am. But I still love him.

SARA   Well, take it from someone who knows, Dawn. Put "Love Me Tender" on your stereo and thank your lucky stars you don't have to wonder where your man is! Thanks for calling.

SARA   *(brightly)*

                Hello, you're on "The Sara Bellum Show." Do you have a question?

TRAVIS   Yes I do. Travis here. My problem is sort of sensitive.

SARA   Nothing is too sensitive for this show, Travis.

TRAVIS   I...I have an addiction.

SARA   Well, you know there's help for you. Have you tried one of those twelve step programs yet?

TRAVIS   It's not alcohol or drugs, Sara. It's chewing gum.

SARA   Chewing gum. Oh, that is a sticky situation.

TRAVIS   Yes, I'm hooked on it. I've got wads of it behind my headboard, I've got it stuck to my dashboard, it's under my bed, on top of my head and my fingers are gooey.

SARA   Travis, just carry a paper bag around to dispose of it.

TRAVIS   There's more. My dentures are stuck together so tight I can't get them in my mouth.

SARA   Try using a little tar and bug remover. That stuff will dissolve anything!

TRAVIS   But I have to put them in my mouth...

SARA   I'm kidding! Plus there's no need to thank me... well, that's all the time we have for today, folks. Thanks for tuning in to "The Sara Bellum Show." If you've got a problem, just ask Sara.

Mardi Gras

Characters:	Gloob, Martian Space Traveler
	Dweek, Martian Space Traveler
	Kris, Mardi Gras Celebrant
	Bill, Mardi Gras Celebrant
Setting:	The Mardi Gras Carnival
Props:	2 long cardboard guns for Martians. The Martians may wear paper helmets.
Hint:	Martians sound like robots

. . . .

KRIS   *(walks toward Martians)*

Hey you guys, great costumes! What are you sup-posed to be, Martians or something?

(touches space suit)

DWEEK   *(points gun)*

Earth people must not touch Dweek's travel garment!

KRIS   Say, you guys have really got the carnival spirit, don't you?

DWEEK   *(thoughtfully)*

Car-ne Vale. From ancient earth language, Latin. Means "farewell to gorging on animal flesh."

BILL   *(pats stomach)*

Ha, ha. After the last two weeks of gorging, we have plenty to say farewell to. By the way, I'm Bill. And this is Kris.

GLOOB   *(points gun)*

Greetings Bill and Kris. Now, you take Gloob and Dweek to your Mardi Gras, the Great Fat Tuesday.

BILL	*(slaps forehead)*
	Oh, my gosh! Kris, I think these two are for real!
KRIS	They're not for real, they're in costume! It's Mardi Gras, remember?
BILL	No. No. They are for real! Look in their eyes. You can see right through their heads!
KRIS	*(gasps)*
	Good grief, you're right! I can! Oh, man! Those have to be the best special effects costumes ever made!
BILL	*(hides mouth with hand)*
	Kris, they're real I tell you!
	(To Martians) Where are you from? How'd you get here?
DWEEK	*(points to sky)*
	We patrol galaxy in our sky rover. We came to warn Earth people of disaster.
KRIS	What disaster?
DWEEK	Computer warns of a forty-day starvation that will befall Earth people, after your time instrument strikes twelve.
BILL	Well, you're sort of right. Our Lent starts at twelve midnight.
GLOOB	Lent? What is meaning of word?
KRIS	Oh boy! And to think my priest had trouble explaining it to me!
BILL	Lent is the time before Easter.
DWEEK	Easter? What is Easter?
KRIS	Easter is the holy day when God's son rose from the dead.

DWEEK   Our computer shows many Earth gods, all hiding be-
                hind false faces. We see Cornus, the god of Mirth.
                Baccus, the god of wine. Many others.

GLOOB   Venus, Goddess of Love. Poseidon, God of the Sea.
                Zeus, Supreme God.

KRIS   No, no. Those gods are only myths. Pretend gods.

GLOOB   Why do Earthmen worship all these pretend gods?

BILL   We don't. Those are people wearing costumes.
                They're part of our Mardi Gras celebration.

DWEEK   Take us to your god of Mardi Gras, the Great Fat
                Tuesday.

KRIS   You guys must be smart, but you've got our lan-
                guage mixed up. Fat Tuesday is from the French.
                Shrove Tuesday is "feast before Lent."

GLOOB   *(points gun)*

                Take us to your Lent.

BILL   No, no. Lent is a time when Earth people don't eat
                meat for 40 days to honor God. The Mardi Gras car-
                nival is a happy time.

DWEEK   Music. Bright colors. Earthlings dance. That means
                happiness?

KRIS   Yes, we're happy. This is a carnival.

GLOOB   That word again. Car-ne-Vale, meaning flesh fare-
                well. A happy time?

KRIS   Yes, it's a tradition that started in 1766 here in
                New Orleans.

BILL   And as our parade moves down Canal Street, peo-
                ple throw coins and beads to other people in the
                crowds.

DWEEK   People like to have things thrown at them?

KRIS   Yes, and we buy cakes with a bean or figure inside
                to eat at king parties.

DWEEK *(points gun)*

Take us to your king.

KRIS I can't. There is no real king.

GLOOB *(points gun)*

Danger, danger, Dweek! A giant winged monster approaches.

DWEEK Monster breathes fire. Prepare for attack. Many monsters follow!

KRIS Put your guns away. Those are floats, to celebrate Mardi Gras.

GLOOB Floats are space ships for Earth people to travel in time?

BILL You guys just don't get it, do you? We don't time-travel or have kings.

DWEEK Earthlings speak with two mouths, like double rocket jets. They starve themselves for one god, yet honor many gods. They are crazy, Gloob.

GLOOB Come, Dweek. We leave this place. Go and find a galaxy with a higher order of being.

DWEEK *(both walk away and Dweek calls over his shoulder)*

Tell the Great Fat Tuesday of disaster. Forty days of starvation in store for Earth people.

Nurse, Come Quick

Characters: Nurse #1
             Nurse #2
             Mr. Brown
             Mrs. Green

Setting: Hospital

Props: None

. . . .

NURSE #1   Good morning, Mr. Brown. Did you ring?

MR. BROWN Yes, I did. I was admitted to this hospital three days ago for observation.

NURSE #1   That's right, Mr. Brown.

MR. BROWN Well, frankly, I'm a little disappointed.

NURSE #1   Why is that, Mr. Brown.

MR. BROWN Well, I've stared at the door, I've looked out the window, and I've checked everybody who goes by, but I still haven't seen a single thing worth observing.

NURSE #1   We'll try to do better, Mr. Brown.

MRS. GREEN Nurse, Nurse, can you come here quick?

NURSE #2   Sure, Miss Green. Are you having a problem?

MRS. GREEN Yes. Every time anybody mentions my name, they say I'm in room 309 and I'm a single.

NURSE #2   That's right, Miss Green. You're in 309 and it's a single room.

MRS. GREEN Why can't anybody here understand anything? I'm Mrs. Green. Not Miss Green. I'm not a single. I'm married.

NURSE #2   I promise to remember that, Mrs. Green.

MR. BROWN Nurse, Nurse, can you come here please?

NURSE #1 Did you ring, Mr. Brown?

MR. BROWN I have a problem. Every time I try to change the channel on my television set, my bed folds up or down.

NURSE #1 How are you trying to change the channel?

MR. BROWN Why, with this doohickey that's attached to the side of my bed, of course.

NURSE #1 Of course. So why don't you just use this little remote on your tray table instead? That should take care of it.

MR. BROWN Oh, OK. I thought that was to make the tray table go up and down.

NURSE #1 No. The tray table stays at that height to fit over your bed.

MR. BROWN Well, thanks for clearing that up, Nurse. Good night.

NURSE #1 Good night, Mr. Brown. Enjoy your television.

MRS. GREEN Nurse, Nurse, can you come here please?

NURSE #2 Did you ring, Mrs. Green?

MRS. GREEN Yes I did. The aide came by and put these little rails up on both sides of my bed. How on earth am I supposed to get out? Climb over?

NURSE #2 You're not supposed to get out. If you need to stand up, please ring and somebody will assist you.

MRS. GREEN That's silly. Why on earth would I need somebody to assist me? I've been getting in and out of bed all my life without help.

NURSE #2 But you're in the hospital now, Mrs. Green. We need to take care of you.

MRS. GREEN I know where I am. You still haven't told me why you think I need help.

NURSE #2   *(sighs)*

It's for your own protection, Mrs. Green. You see, the designers of these hospital gowns forgot to sew up the back seam. And we like to make sure you have it fastened before you stand up.

MRS. GREEN Oh, why didn't you say so in the first place?

NURSE #2   We'll try to do better, Mrs. Green. Good night.

MRS. GREEN Good night.

NURSE #1   This has been a long day.

NURSE #2   Yeah, I know. I must have walked that hall a hundred times.

NURSE #1   Sometimes I wonder why I went into nursing.

NURSE #2   Because you like to work weekends and holidays?

NURSE #1   Nah, that can't be the real reason. Maybe I just like the spirit of adventure.

NURSE #2   Like the adventure of fighting off wild viruses?

NURSE #1   That's it! And instead of a spear, I use my trusty hypodermic needle.

NURSE #2   *(teasingly)*

And you're doing a fine job of it.

NURSE #1   By the way, Dr. Smiley is moving Miss Green from 309 down to the rehabilitation center today.

NURSE #2   That's great. She must be getting better. I'm going to miss that lady.

NURSE #1   Me too.

NURSE #2   And by the way, it's *MRS.* Green, not Miss. She's not a single, she's married, you know.

NURSE #1   *(thoughtfully)*

Hmmm, I wonder who's coming into 309 now?

Plain Vanilla, Please

Characters: Clerk
              Customer #1
              Customer #2

Setting: An ice cream shop

Props: Order pad and pencil

. . . .

CLERK   Hi, folks. What'll you have?

CUSTOMER #1   I'll have two scoops of vanilla ice cream please.

CUSTOMER #2   That sounds good. I'll have the same.

CLERK   OK!

                   (writes)

                   Two scoops of vanilla for each. Good choice.

                   (pauses)

                   Will that be on a cone or a dish?

CUSTOMER #1   I haven't had a cone in ages. I'll have a cone.

CUSTOMER #2   I'll take mine in a dish.

CLERK   Super. A cone and a dish.

                   (looks at Customer #1)

                   Do you want a sugar cone or a cake cone?

                   (puts pencil to pad)

CUSTOMER #1   Oh, gosh. What's the light tan cone? Is that a
                   sugar or a cake?

CLERK   That would be the cake.

CUSTOMER #1   OK. Make it a cake cone.

CLERK   Terrific. One cake cone. Do you want the point
                      ed bottom or the flat bottom?

CUSTOMER #1   Hmmm. Well, I could set it down if it was flat.
                      But, no. A cone has a point. So make it a pointed
                      cone.

CLERK   Alright, one pointed cake cone with two scoops
                      of vanilla.

                      (holds pencil up)

                      And as for the dish. Will you be having a topping
                      on those two scoops of vanilla?

CUSTOMER #2   Topping? That would be nice. What do you have?

CLERK   Let's see. There's chocolate, marshmallow,
                      butterscotch, strawberry, cherry, orange,
                      coconut, crushed pineapple...

CUSTOMER #2   Go no further! I'll have chocolate topping.

CLERK   Great choice!

                      (pauses)

                      Do you prefer regular chocolate or hot fudge?

CUSTOMER #2   Hot fudge sounds good.

CLERK   Excellent. And will you want sprinkles on that?
                      Or nuts?

CUSTOMER #2   Make it nuts.

CLERK   Nuts it is. Walnuts? Peanuts? Pecans? Hazelnuts?

CUSTOMER #2   Surprise me.

CLERK   OK. A nut surprise. Now, back to the cone. Would
                      you like the ice cream rolled in one of our
                      delicious sprinkles?

CUSTOMER #1   Such as?

CLERK	We have crushed M & M's, chocolate chips, cookie crumbs, rainbow sprinkles, or plain chocolate hard shell topping.
CUSTOMER #1	Give me the hard shell.
CLERK	Hard shell it is. And back to the dish—would you like that topped with whipped cream?
CUSTOMER #2	Yes. Lots of it.
CLERK	You're the boss!
CUSTOMER #1	Fine. Now, if you'll just get the ice cream...
CLERK	Coming right up. And by the way, would you like anything to drink with that?
CUSTOMER #1	No, nothing for me.
CUSTOMER #2	I'll have some water, please.
CUSTOMER #1	Yeah, water sounds good. I'll have some too.
CLERK	Two waters it is. Would you prefer those waters with a straw or without?
CUSTOMER #1	Yes. No. Whatever. Could you just get the...?
CLERK	Oh, one more thing. How about a nice red cherry on top of your ice cream?
CUSTOMER #2	*(exasperated)*
	Yes! Now, will you please just get it for us?
CLERK	You bet! Coming right up.
	(starts to walk away, turns and asks...)
	By the way, would you like ice with your water?
CUSTOMER #1	Yes! Yes! Yes! Yes to ice water. Yes to ice cream. Yes or I'll scream!
CLERK	*(walks away mumbling)*
	Some customers are so hard to please.

Please Press One

Characters: Phone (Voice)
             Mrs. Smith

Setting: Mrs. Smith's house

Props: Telephone and a prescription bottle

. . . .

MRS. SMITH *(calmly looks at bottle)*

I'm out of my sedative medicine. Hmmm. The bottle says I can call the pharmacy's time saving refill service. Great. That'll save time.

(says numbers aloud as she presses them)

555-2061

PHONE Hello. You have reached the Get Well Pharmacy. Please listen for your options. If you know your party's extension, please enter it now. If you wish to talk to our front register, please press 1. If this is a doctor's office, please press 2. If you wish to use our time saving refill service, please press 3.

MRS. SMITH I want a refill...

(presses and speaks)

3

PHONE You have pressed 3 for a refill. Please enter the 6-digit prescription number which is located at the upper left of your prescription bottle.

MRS. SMITH OK.

(presses and speaks numbers)

9, 8, 2, 3, 0, 4

PHONE   You have pressed 9, 8, 2, 3, 0, 4. If this is correct, press 1. If this is incorrect, press 2.

MRS. SMITH   *(presses and speaks)*

1

PHONE   You have indicated that this number is correct. The first three initials of the patient's last name are S-M-I. If this is correct, please press 1. If this is incorrect, please press 2.

MRS. SMITH   *(presses and speaks)*

1

PHONE   Your prescription will be refilled by our time saving refill service. If you wish to pick up your prescription today, please press 1. If you wish to pick up your prescription tomorrow, please press 2.

MRS. SMITH   *(presses and speaks)*

1

PHONE   You have indicated that you wish to pick up your prescription today. Please enter the time of day you wish to pick it up.

MRS. SMITH   *(presses and speaks)*

OK. 10:30. 1, 0, 3, 0

PHONE   You have indicated that you wish to pick up your prescription at 10:30. If you wish to pick it up in the A.M., please press 1. If you wish to pick it up in the P.M., please press 2.

MRS. SMITH   *(sighs and presses)*

1

PHONE   You have indicated you wish to pick up your prescription number 982304 at 10:30 A.M. Please hold while we check the availability of your prescription.

MRS. SMITH *(exasperated)*

OK, OK. I'm holding, I'm holding.

PHONE   Thank you for holding. This is your Get Well Pharmacy's time saving refill service. The prescription refill you have ordered is temporarily out of stock.

MRS. SMITH *(moans)*

Out of stock!

PHONE   If you wish to have your Get Well Pharmacy's time saving refill service reorder this prescription for you, please press 1. If you wish to speak to a pharmacist about the length of time a reorder will require, please press 2. If you wish to inquire about a substitute medication, please contact your physician's office.

MRS. SMITH OK, OK. I'll speak to a pharmacist.

(presses and speaks)

2

PHONE   You have indicated you would like to speak to a pharmacist. Both of our pharmacists are busy serving other patients at this time. Your call is important to us. Please continue to hold. We are sorry for the inconvenience.

MRS. SMITH *(shrieks)*

It's important to me, too. OK. I'll hold.

PHONE   *(click!)*

MRS. SMITH No. No. No. I've been cut off!

(slams the phone down)

Well, I'll just call the doctor and have him order a substitute prescription.

(presses numbers for doctor's office)

PHONE   You have reached Dr. Wintergreen's office. All of
                   our lines are busy at the present time but your
                   call IS important to us. Please hold the line.

MRS. SMITH   And I thought I needed a sedative prescription
                   before!

Procedures, Procedures

Characters: Miss Stickler, Receptionist
             Mr. Drainwell
             Mrs. Trembley
             Mr. Healey
             Mrs. Hytense

Setting: A busy doctor's office

Props: A clip board and a pencil

. . . .

**MR.
DRAINWELL** Good morning. I'm Joe Drainwell. The doctor is ex-
           pecting me.

**MISS
STICKLER** Just sign in on this clipboard and complete these
            insurance forms.

**MR.
DRAINWELL** That shouldn't be necessary. I spoke to the doctor
           just a few minutes ago. He asked me to come in.

**MISS
STICKLER** It's procedure. You must sign the clipboard.

**MR.
DRAINWELL** Oh, OK.

           (signs)

**MISS
STICKLER** Fine. May I see your insurance card while you fill
            in the forms?

**MR.
DRAINWELL** The doctor won't need my insurance card. He told
           me to come in.

**MISS
STICKLER** Nobody sees the doctor without an insurance card.
            It's procedure.

MR.
DRAINWELL Why do you want my insurance card?

MISS
STICKLER *(huffily)*

Why, to assure payment, of course.

MR.
DRAINWELL Then, you'd better show me his card. I'm here to fix the plumbing.

MISS
STICKLER Oh, in that case, go right in!

MRS.
TREMBLEY Here you are, Miss Stickler. I finished the forms.

MISS
STICKLER Thank you Mrs. Trembley.

(looks at form)

But you didn't say why you came to see the doctor. Why are you here?

MRS.
TREMBLEY Must I tell you? The doctor will just ask me again.

MISS
STICKLER It's procedure. I have to have all the blanks filled in.

MRS.
TREMBLEY Oh, very well. I suppose it won't hurt to say. I came to see him because I've been so nervous lately.

MISS
STICKLER Nervous? My goodness you look fine. What's making you nervous?

MRS.
TREMBLEY Everything! Sometimes I just fall to pieces.

MISS
STICKLER Well, pull yourself together and have a seat. The doctor will be with you soon.

MISS STICKLER   Why, hello there, Mr. Healey. We haven't seen you in a long time.

MR. HEALEY   I know. The last time I was here something made me leery of ever coming back.

MISS STICKLER   My goodness! Whatever was it?

MR. HEALEY   Well, while I was in the waiting room, I noticed everybody there was sick with something or other.

MISS STICKLER   Yes, that's why they come to the doctor. They're all sick.

MR. HEALEY   But people were sneezing and sniffing and spreading germs.

MISS STICKLER   Now, don't you worry about germs. The doctor will be just fine. He protects himself with rubber gloves. Go right in.

MISS HYTENSE   *(signs pad)*

Boy, do I hate coming to the doctor!

MISS STICKLER   Sorry to hear that. May I see your insurance card, please?

MISS HYTENSE   Of course. But that's why I hate it. Everything is so impersonal these days. Nobody gets special attention or sympathy any more.

MISS STICKLER   OK, I'll go along with that. Why do you need sympathy?

MISS HYTENSE   Oh, I just feel uneasy having an examination. I'm afraid of what the doctor might find.

MISS STICKLER Now, don't you worry about that. I've worked for the doctor for twenty years and he hasn't found a thing yet.

MISS HYTENSE You really know how to make a person feel better!

MISS STICKLER Thank you. Please have a seat.

MISS STICKLER *(motions to Mrs. Trembley)*

Could you come back over here a minute? Line 53 on your form isn't clear about whether you or any family member has had high blood pressure.

MRS. TREMBLEY Sure it is. It asks if I or either of my parents has had high blood pressure. I simply wrote "N-A" for "Not Applicable."

MISS STICKLER Well, "N-A" is not good enough. We must have a complete medical history if we are to treat you in this office. That's procedure.

MRS. TREMBLEY Very well. I'll change it to read "No."

MISS STICKLER OK. And you left line 72 blank...the one that asks if either parent had any hereditary illnesses. We need a complete record.

MRS. TREMBLEY *(sighs)*

Very well. I'll write "No" on that line too.

MISS STICKLER *(points to form)*

Section B asks you to describe in detail all of the surgeries you have had. The section must be filled in. That's procedure.

MRS. TREMBLEY   But I haven't had any surgeries.

MISS STICKLER   Oh. Well then. Just write "N-A" for "Not Applicable" and let's get you into the examination room.

MRS. TREMBLEY   OK. But let me change line 53 first. My blood pressure just went up!

The Voter Speaks

Characters:	Philip Regent, Show Host
	Tanya Reed, Assistant
	Zachary Taylor, Contestant
Setting:	Set of the game show, "The Voter Speaks"
Props:	Box with slips of paper in it, pan and spoon to clang, key chain.

....

PHILIP   Ladies and gentlemen! Welcome! Welcome to the country's hottest new game show, "The Voter Speaks." I'm your host, Philip Regent, and this is my lovely assistant, Tanya Reed.

TANYA   *(gives flirty smile)*

Thanks, Philip. Can't you just feel the electricity crackling tonight here in the nation's capital? It's crackling!

PHILIP   That's right, Tanya. Now let's meet our new contestant, Zachary Taylor. Zachary, are you ready to play "The Voter Speaks?"

ZACHARY   Oh yeah! I'm primed. I got my Masters Degree in Government.

PHILIP   Then you're on the right show, Zachary, because our questions are based on the U.S. government. But first, may I ask, how did you get your name?

ZACHARY   Easy. Our family's name is Taylor and my father was history buff, so he named me after old President Number Twelve.

PHILIP   Let's hope the name brings you luck. Now, let's review the rules.

ZACHARY   OK.

| PHILIP | Your first correct answer wins you $1,000. You can take your winnings and quit, or play and double your money with every right answer. A wrong answer loses everything. Are you ready, Zach? |

| ZACHARY | Ready! Government is my bag. |

| PHILIP | OK, Zach. Tanya has a box of questions on the government. Draw one. |

| TANYA | *(offers the box)* |

Here you are, and goooood luck!

| ZACHARY | *(draws a slip and hands it to Philip)* |

I can't believe this! My category is Presidents! It's my specialty!

| PHILIP | We're off to a good start. Now, Zachary, for $1,000: Name the first five presidents of the United States of America in order. |

| ZACHARY | Piece of cake! George Washington, John Adams, Thomas Jefferson, James Madison and James Monroe. |

| TANYA | Yeahhh! That's $1,000 big ones, Zachary. Are you still in, or do you take the thousand and fold? |

| ZACHARY | Are you kidding? I'm in! |

| PHILIP | OK. But you know it's double or nothing. Tanya, the box please. |

| TANYA | *(holds the box out)* |

Here you are, Zachary. Pick a good one.

| ZACHARY | *(draws a slip and hands it to Philip)* |

| PHILIP | OK, for double or nothing: Who were the next three presidents and what years did they serve? |

| ZACHARY | *(smugly)* |

John Quincy Adams, from 1825 to 1829
Andrew Jackson, from 1829 to 1837 and
Martin Van Buren, from 1837 to 1841

TANYA	Right again! Right again! That brings you to $2,000. Are you still in?
ZACHARY	*(nods)*
	I'm in!
	(draws a slip and hands it to Philip)
PHILIP	Oh, this is a tough one. For $4,000: Name the presidents who died in office.
ZACHARY	Tough? Ha! I cut my teeth on these facts. There were eight: William Henry Harrison Zachary Taylor, ha ha, does that name sound familiar? Abraham Lincoln James Garfield William McKinley Warren G. Harding Franklin D. Roosevelt, and John F. Kennedy
TANYA	You're sizzling, Zachary. Sizzling. Are you still in for $8,000?
ZACHARY	Ha, ha. I'm playing in my court!
	(draws a slip and hands it to Philip)
PHILIP	That's what we like to hear. OK, Zach the next one is on your namesake.
ZACHARY	Am I lucky, or what?
PHILIP	Zachary Taylor was born a southerner but as president, he took a hard line against the South. Some historians speculate that if he had not died in office, he might have prevented...what?
ZACHARY	Being buried? No, ha ha. A joke. He might have prevented the U.S. Civil War.
TANYA	Oh, this guy is sparkling. Sparkling! Do you want to take your $8,000 and go home now, Zachary? Or are you sticking with us?

ZACHARY   Sticking like Super Glue!

                (draws a slip and hands it to Philip)

PHILIP   For $16,000: Which president ushered in the twen-
                tieth century?

ZACHARY   Old Number 25, William McKinley.

                (grabs next question)

TANYA   Oh, this man is lightning. Lightning!

PHILIP   OK, for $32,000: What are the President's official
                duties?

ZACHARY   He's chief executive officer of the government,
                head of the executive branch and commander in
                chief of the armed forces.

TANYA   *(shrieks)*

                Wow! Zach is cool. Cool!

                (holds out box)

                You're still in?

ZACHARY   *(draws a slip and hands it to Philip)*

                Still in!

TANYA   Ohhhh! He's still in for 64 thousand! Good luck,
                Zachary!

PHILIP   OK, looks like we're easing off the tough ones.
                What are the requirements to be president?

ZACHARY   Easy. He must be a natural born citizen of the
                U.S., 35 years old or older, and must have been a
                resident of the U.S. for at least 14 years.

TANYA   Oh, you're hot, hot, hot. And for $128,000! I'm
                getting nervous.

PHILIP   All those years of studying government are paying
                off. Are you still in?

ZACHARY   Gimme that slip!

(draws a slip and hands it to Philip)

PHILIP   Oh man, this is too good to be true! Fate is with you today, buddy. For $256,000: Name the current president of the United States!

ZACHARY   Current? Like now?! Uh...

(shakes his head and gulps)

Just a minute. I know this one. I've got it.

PHILIP   Ten more seconds, Zachary. For $256,000! You can do it!

ZACHARY   It's on the tip of my tongue.

TANYA   *(bangs the gong)*

PHILIP   Ohhhhh, I'm sorry. Time's up! Oh, Zachary you were so close.

ZACHARY   I know it! Wait! Wait! I've got it!

PHILIP   *(pats Zachary on back)*

You've been a terrific contestant, Zachary! Thanks for playing "The Voter Speaks." Do we have a consolation prize for this tough competitor, Tanya?

TANYA   *(holds up prize)*

We sure do have, Philip. A key chain with a charm of the White House on it!

ZACHARY   *(screams)*

Mommy! I want my mommy!

Who Wants To Look Silly?

Characters: Hilbert Haslett, Game Host
              JoAnn Blakley, Contestant
              Cletus Blakley (JoAnn's brother), sits to side of stage
              with phone.

Setting: Stage of the game show, "Who Wants To Look Silly?"

Prop: Phone

. . . .

HILBERT   Audience, one of you will be our next contestant.
              Put the following events in the right order and
              hit the buzzer on the arm of your chair. First one
              correct wins. (A) The Stone Age (B) Man Walks on
              Moon (C) The Renaissance (D) Now

JOANN   *(makes buzzer noise)*

              I hope it's me!

HILBERT   There's the buzzer! The right order is A, C, B, D.
              And the lady in seat number 92 got it right. Seat
              92, come on up here!

JOANN   *(rushes to Hilbert)*

              Oh, it's me, it's me!

HILBERT   Congratulations! And you are...?

JOANN   JoAnn Blakley from Pennsylvania.

HILBERT   OK, JoAnn. Without further ado, for $100: If you
              were a monkey, what would be your favorite food?
              (A) burgers and fries, (B) raw fish, (C) bananas,
              or (D) ice cream?

JOANN   If I were a monkey...hmmmm. All your questions are
              trick questions, so I have to be careful.

HILBERT   Ha ha, it looks like you're onto us, JoAnn. So,
              you think this is a trick question, do you?

JOANN	Well, yeah. Let's see. Where was this monkey born? Is he allergic to bananas? Oh, dear. This is a tough one. My brother, Cletus, is a veterinarian. May I call him?
HILBERT	Sure, our operator will connect you.
JOANN	*(pauses)*
	Hello, Cletus? I made it onto the show. Are you watching?
CLETUS	Yes. And you're right, it could be a trick. That's why they call it "Who Wants To Look Silly?" And what about the possibility that the monkey's owner runs a fast food joint? That could be the case...
JOANN	That's true! Then, he'd like burgers and fries.
HILBERT	Is that your answer, JoAnn...A, burgers and fries?
JOANN	I'm not sure. Cletus, what do you think?
CLETUS	Maybe he's part of the show at Water World. They'd give him fish.
JOANN	Then there's the obvious—most monkeys eat bananas. But this one may dislike the heat of tropical climates and want something cold like ice cream. What do you think the answer is, Cletus?
CLETUS	I can't decide for you, JoAnn. It's a dilemma.
JOANN	OK. I'm going to poll the audience.
HILBERT	Audience, JoAnn needs your help. The voting buttons are on the arm of your chair.
	(pauses)
	OK. Let's see what the audience says. 67% say "A"...10% say "B"...and 23% say "D."
JOANN	Well, I was about to go with C—bananas. But not one person in the audience said bananas. So I'll go with A: burgers and fries.

HILBERT   There's only one way to settle this. Pull the curtain and let's see what the real monkey goes for.

(Pauses)

OK. There he goes. He's heading for the...for the ...bananas! He's peeling it. He's putting it in his mouth. It's bananas.

JOANN   Oh, dear. I should have said bananas.

HILBERT   But you didn't! You thought it was a trick question. BOY, DO YOU LOOK SILLY!

JOANN   Darned monkey.

HILBERT   Too bad, JoAnn, but nice try. Now, audience, one of you will be our next contestant. I'll give you a question and the first to get it right wins a spot on "Who Wants To Look Silly?"

JOANN   *(walks offstage mumbling)*

And no matter what...you will look silly!

Won't You Come Home?

Characters: Tillie, hairdresser with mirror and comb
              Lil, customer in chair
              Josh, hairdresser with mirror and comb
              Dee, customer in chair

Setting: The beauty salon

Props: Two combs, two mirrors, two chairs

. . . .

TILLIE   *(stands behind Lil, pretending to comb her hair)*

I love the way this style looks on you, Lil. It's modern and very youthful.

(hands Lil a mirror)

LIL   Thanks, Tillie. I like it too, but don't you think you should comb a few hairs down across my forehead to soften the look a little bit?

TILLIE   OK. But not enough to give you bangs. Bangs are definitely yesterday!

JOSH   *(nods toward Lil)*

Definitely yesterday! That's why I've combed Dee's hair away from her face at the temples. She looks a lot like Diane Sawyer now, don't you think?

(shows Dee a mirror)

DEE   Diane Sawyer?

(looks in mirror)

She's my favorite. Maybe with this new look, a certain somebody will get over his roving eye and pay some attention to me.

JOSH   Ohhhh! Your guy is one of that kind, is he?

DEE   *(sadly)*

I'm afraid so. And after I've given him the best
two months of my life.

JOSH   Well, then. I'd say give the bum the bum's rush.
Get rid of him!

DEE   I wish it were that easy. I noticed him looking at
another woman and I told him I never wanted to see
him again. Now, I wish I hadn't said that.

TILLIE   No one but you can decide what you want to do,
Dee. But in my opinion, if you think you want to
get him back, you've gotta fight fire with fire.

LIL   Personally, I would apply the fire to his shoes and
see how fast he can run—in the opposite direction!

TILLIE   Now, Lil. It's Dee's decision. If she wants to keep
this guy, we should give her all the support we can.

LIL   Well, you and Josh are in the right business to
help her, that's for sure. There must be a million
dollars worth of beauty products on those shelves.

JOSH   And we know how to use them!

               (walks over to Dee and stares at her face)

Let's start by emphasizing those gorgeous eyes
with some artfully applied Andre' Fabulon mascara
and spring lilac shadow.

TILLIE   Good idea. And some mauve blush to highlight her
cheekbones.

LIL   *(gets up and walks over to Dee)*

I see what you mean. They are nice cheekbones.
What would you think of a lipstick with a faint
violet tint?

JOSH   Perfect! She will be the breath of springtime.

TILLIE   You need to wear jewelry to complement the plum
tones in your makeup, Dee. I guarantee he won't be
able to take his eyes off of you.

DEE   Hey, you guys. I'm grateful for all this attention you're giving me, and I know you mean well. But he isn't going to see the results of your work if he is nowhere around.

JOSH   Then there's only one thing for you to do, sweetie. You get yourself all prettied up and go to the telephone. Dial his number and when he answers, you just tell him:

(starts singing, motioning all to join in)

ALL   *Won't you come home, Bill Bailey?*
Won't you come home?
She moaned the whole day long.
I'll do the cooking, honey. I'll pay the rent.
I know I've done you wrong.

Remember that rainy evening I drove you out?
With nothing but a fine tooth comb?
I know I'm to blame. Well ain't that a shame?
Bill Bailey won't you please come home?

(repeat)

A Birthday Roast

(Note to Activity Director: This skit is better suited for a male resident with a birthday)

Characters: This skit can be read by two or three participants, or let numerous participants in the group take turns. Use the blanks to fill in the birthday boy's name.

Setting: The social room

Props: None

. . . .

SPEAKER 1: Today is _____'s birthday. Be nice to him. Or...maybe not. He may start to expect it.

SPEAKER 2: _____ has been working out lately. His favorite exercise is lifting the remote.

SPEAKER 3: But sometimes he misses his workout session when his cat is sleeping on it.

SPEAKER 4: We won't say how old _____ is but let's just say that God called him a rough draft.

SPEAKER 5: _____ never learned to swim. Noah assured him the boat wouldn't sink.

SPEAKER 6: We're not picking on _____'s age, but he still has the card he got on his twenty-first birthday. It said "Your request for a leave is granted. Signed, General Custer."

SPEAKER 7: _____ went to the doctor complaining of a pain in his eye. The doctor suggested he take the spoon out of his cup before drinking from it.

SPEAKER 8: _____ always believed that when the going gets tough, it's time for a coffee break.

SPEAKER 9: _____ used to be a dog breeder. He once tried to cross a Spitz with a Chow-Chow. He ended up with a Spitz-Chow. It was a nice dog, but it threw up a lot.

SPEAKER 10: _____ always claimed that its barf was worse than its bite.

SPEAKER 11: _____ first decided he wanted to be an accountant when somebody told him he would get to stare at figures all day.

SPEAKER 12: But he quit when he realized there are only three kinds of accountants in the world...those who can count and those who can't.

SPEAKER 13: Then he decided he wanted to work in a pharmacy. But he gave that up when he couldn't figure out how to get those little bottles into the typewriter.

SPEAKER 14: _____ is like a transmission with three speeds: Idle, slow, and slower.

SPEAKER 15: Have you noticed that the only time _____ speeds up is on his way to the dining room?

SPEAKER 16: And watch your plate if he sits near you at dinner. He thinks that food eaten off someone else's plate doesn't have any calories.

SPEAKER 17: Has _____ been offering you candy bars every time you see him? He thinks if he fattens everybody else up, he's going to look thinner by comparison.

SPEAKER 18: Have you noticed how great _____ looks? He's been on the Cancel Out Diet. He believes the calories in cake are cancelled out by the zero calories in a diet soda.

SPEAKER 19: We all wish you a very happy birthday, and many more to come!

(everybody joins in to sing the Happy Birthday Song)

A Kinder, Gentler Birthday Wish

(Note to Activity Director: This skit is better suited for a female resident with a birthday)

Characters: This skit can be read by two or three participants, or let nine different participants take turns. Use the blank to fill in the birthday girl's name.

Setting: The social room

Props: None

. . . .

SPEAKER 1: Every one of us here wants to join in wishing _____ a Happy Birthday.

SPEAKER 2: If we had a sash, we could place it across her shoulder and declare her to be Miss Congeniality.

SPEAKER 3: If we had a crown, we would place it on her head and make her Queen for A Day.

SPEAKER 4: She has worn many hats and played many parts in her life. If we had a chef's hat, we could place it on her head to honor the thousands of meals she has cooked for others.

SPEAKER 5: Or a nurse's cap, to point out the countless times she has given comfort to someone who was in need.

SPEAKER 6: Or a chauffeur's cap to honor the times she has gone out of her way to help someone else.

SPEAKER 7: Or an artist's beret to show how she uses her talents to make our surroundings more attractive.

SPEAKER 8: But what we *DO* have is a birthday cake with candles to symbolize how she makes everything she touches a little brighter.

SPEAKER 9: So we ask everybody to join us in singing Happy Birthday.

(everybody joins in to sing the Happy Birthday Song)

Section 5

Resident Life and Reality Checks

Con Artists

Characters: Vera Van Deusen, Chair of Meeting
              Sgt. Stan Strong, Police Officer
              Sonja
              Max
              Kay

Setting: A meeting at the Shady Acres Retirement Center

Props: None

. . . .

VERA   Welcome everybody. We've called this meeting to
            alert our seniors to the many con artists at work
            today. Our guest is Sgt. Stan Strong of the city
            police department.

SGT. STAN   Thanks, Vera. As all of you know, it's a common
            belief that senior citizens have money. Lots of
            money. And there are a lot of people out there who
            will be glad to help you get rid of it.

VERA   So, Sgt. Strong, are you going to talk about some
            simple ways we can be alert to their scams?

SGT. STAN   Yes. One of the most common ways they get your
            confidence is to call you and use your name. Then
            they ask how you are. Something like "Hello Mrs.
            Walker. How are you today?" Does that sound familiar?

SONJA   *(raises hand)*

            It happened to me just today. But I didn't fall
            for it.

SGT. STAN   What did you say?

SONJA   I said, "Oh, I feel terrible. My ears hurt and my
            teeth ache and my temperature is a hundred and
            eight. And every time I take a bite of food I get
            the most awful pain in my stomach."

VERA   Good job, Sonja. What happened next?

SONJA	The guy said, "Uh, I'll call later," and he hung up on me! Next time, I'll just hang up on him first.
SGT. STAN	Actually that's what we recommend you do, Sonja. The instant you realize it's any kind of sales pitch, hang up.
MAX	*(raises hand)*
	The last guy who called me started by telling me exactly what kind of vitamins I use! I thought he might be from the drug store, so I asked him how he knew.
SGT. STAN	And then did he just smoothly ease the conversation into trying to sell you a lot of supplements you didn't need?
MAX	Yes.
SGT. STAN	Again, the best response would be to hang up. Then call your pharmacy yourself if you have questions.
KAY	*(raises hand)*
	That's scary! Don't we have any privacy left in this world?
VERA	Sadly, very little. Some organizations gather information and sell it to other organizations that build profiles. They learn what we buy, where we go, even private things about us, like our financial information.
KAY	Well, I tested that idea once. I filled out a questionnaire that came with a hair dryer warranty. I filled it in and said I liked sports. Told them I liked surfing, scuba diving, and mountain climbing.
SGT. STAN	How long was it before someone offered you a vacation in Hawaii?
KAY	*(gasps)*
	How did you know? It was less than a month.
SGT. STAN	That's how they operate. Do you remember exactly what they offered?

KAY	Sure. Two weeks in Honolulu. They would pay for the hotel and dinner every evening. All I had to do was pay for the plane tickets.
SGT. STAN	Are you aware that if you had gone, they would have had salesmen at those dinners trying to get you to buy property or time-shares, or insist you make investments?
VERA	Remember people, you've heard this before, but it's true. There are no free meals.
SGT. STAN	It's dangerous to get involved with mail order contests, too. Has anybody here ever fallen for one of those?
MAX	*(raises hand)* I entered a poetry contest. I sent in a poem and a ten dollar entry fee.
VERA	And did you win?
MAX	No, they sent me a congratulations letter telling me how talented I am. And they said if I'd send twenty more dollars they would publish my poem in a book of poetry. Naturally, I threw it away.
SONJA	Why does everybody deliberately try to cheat people?
SGT. STAN	Some of them may be OK. But lots of them are thieves. It's as simple as that. They know that many seniors are lonely people and will let them start talking. The best thing is to not let them start.
VERA	Very often, seniors don't want to be rude, so they don't hang up on the caller. But be rude! You didn't ask them to call. They're bothering you with the intention of taking advantage of you.
KAY	I feel so foolish because I've answered so many of those warranty questionnaires with the right information about myself.
SGT. STAN	Don't feel foolish. Learn from it. Even I got taken for a ride by a roofing contractor once.

VERA   You, Sergeant?

SGT. STAN   Yes. He gave me an estimate. A little later, he
                came back and said that because my roof was so
                bad, he had gotten an emergency permit for a new
                roof. All I had to do was give him a down payment
                and he'd start work the next day.

VERA   I know what's coming.

SGT. STAN   *(nods)*

                Well, I thought about it and called City Hall.
                They said he hadn't applied for a permit. Then I
                called The Good Business Association, and they
                said the guy was a crook. So I stopped payment on
                my check.

KAY   OK, now I don't feel so bad.

VERA   The moral is: Nice guys not only finish last, they
                often lose their life savings to scam artists. So
                be alert.

SGT. STAN   And never let anybody rush you into signing any-
                thing before you are absolutely certain that
                you're doing the right thing. Ask an expert before
                you sign anything.

VERA   But what if I really want to give to a worthy
                charity?

SGT. STAN   Give to whoever you like. But remember, most char-
                ities only get about five percent of what is so-
                licited by phone. You'd be better off sending a
                check directly to the charity's main office.

KAY   Maybe it's best to take the time to think before
                agreeing to anything.

                *(Kay, Sonja and Max nod in agreement and murmur
                amongst themselves)*

Cruisin'

Characters: Diana
             Sadie
             Dwight

Setting: The social room at High Cliffs Residence

Props: None

. . . .

DIANA   What's the matter, Sadie? You look a little down.

SADIE   Oh, I'm OK. Just feeling a little blue today.

DWIGHT   It's probably the post-holiday doldrums. Everybody
               gets them.

SADIE   I guess so. It seems everybody did their visiting
               in December and now that it's January, nobody is
               even phoning me.

DIANA   I'm glad to get a chance to rest. After all the
               holiday hustle and bustle, I'm happy for a bit of
               a break.

DWIGHT   Sadie, if you're lonesome, why don't you pick up
               the phone and do the calling yourself?

SADIE   I could. But maybe all my family and friends want
               to relax, like Diana said.

DIANA   I have an idea. Why not go on a vacation?

DWIGHT   That always works for me.

SADIE   *(sighs)*

               My doctor wouldn't want me to go away just yet.
               Not so soon after surgery.

DWIGHT   Well then, I have an idea. How about a cruise?

SADIE   Dwight, you don't understand. My doctor...

DWIGHT   I don't mean a real cruise. Let's plan an imaginary cruise.

DIANA   Great idea. We'll all take part in one. Let's have a party with a cruise theme.

SADIE   Sounds good to me! Let's name our imaginary ship the Bye Bye Blues Cruise Line.

DIANA   I love the name! Dwight, will you be the ship's captain?

DWIGHT   Sure. I'll wear my blue blazer and get a yacht cap.

SADIE   We'll play island music. And we'll have seafood for refreshments.

DWIGHT   Would you like to go to the Caribbean? The air is always balmy and the sky is a perfect blue. And at night, the stars are so low you can almost touch them.

DIANA   You've been there before, haven't you Dwight?

DWIGHT   A couple of times. I'll get my pictures to give us some ideas for the decorations.

SADIE   Even an imaginary cruise has to have music for dancing. We'll encourage the people in wheelchairs to sway in their chairs.

DIANA   I'll make invitations and tickets. Let's start right away so people can get their flowered shirts and cruise wear ready.

DWIGHT   This is fun. I've got a million ideas.

SADIE   You know something. My blues are gone!

DIANA   Thanks to the Bye Bye Blues Cruise Line.

SADIE   I can't wait to set sail.

Dixie in My Heart

Characters: Two to twelve people. Take turns reading.

Setting: The activity room of a retirement home.

Props: None

. . . .

SPEAKER 1   There's a blizzard going on outside. The streets are all closed, so we can't go anywhere. The radio says it's a state of emergency. So we'll just have to have some fun in here where it's warm.

SPEAKER 2   Well then, there's only one thing left for us to do. Let's go on a trip in our imaginations. We'll go anywhere we want. Any time of year. Pick a place and tell everybody about it.

SPEAKER 3   OK. I think I'll go to San Francisco to see the ocean. There's nothing like the sound of the waves breaking on the shore! Ahhh, that fresh air! And it's so pretty when the sun breaks through the clouds after a rain.

SPEAKER 4   I grew up in Ohio. Near Columbus. I'll go there. It's August and a hot, dry breeze is rustling through the cornfields. Ohio people are so friendly. We'll have a corn roast after the sun goes down and everybody will come.

SPEAKER 5   It's July and I'm on a Mississippi paddle wheeler. I'll get on at Cape Girardeau and sail on down to New Orleans. There's a jazz band and I'm sipping a cool iced tea. The boat is rocking. Kids on the shore are waving to us.

SPEAKER 6   I'm going on a long car ride through the Rockies. I want to see the fog hanging over the hilltops and watch the morning sun burn it off. The air is fresh and clear. An eagle is circling slowly. He's riding an air current like a sailboat.

SPEAKER 7 Since we're getting away from this blizzard, I'll go all the way to the desert out in Arizona. I'm riding a beautiful chestnut stallion. There are purple hills in the distance. Tiny red flowers are blooming on the cactus plants. And a little armadillo is standing perfectly still in the sand, watching us go by.

SPEAKER 8 I'm in Paris in the springtime. Pear trees are budding and the flower vendors have set up their stalls on the sidewalks. The smell of fresh baked French bread is wafting through the open doors of the bakeries. I'll buy some paints and an easel and sit at an outdoor café and paint.

SPEAKER 9 I'm going to London to watch the changing of the guard at Buckingham Palace. The Queen will ride by in her carriage and wave her white glove at me. She'll tell her coachman to stop and invite me to ride with her. She'll tell me she's always wanted to talk with one of the common folk who line the roadside.

SPEAKER 10 I'll go to Hollywood and watch them make a movie. They'll send out a call for extras, and I'll get to sit in for a scene or two. I'll meet some famous movie stars. Then I'll watch for the movie to come out and look for myself on the screen. Won't that be fun!

SPEAKER 11 Maybe I'll go to the Grand Canyon and ride a little donkey down one of the steep paths to the bottom. I've always wanted to be adventurous. And I'll buy an Indian blanket to hang on my wall. Then I'll decorate my room around the colors.

SPEAKER 12 Well, I hope you guys all have a good time. But me, I'm just going to sit here in this room and watch the snow fall. And I'll remember growing up in the South where it was warm and sunny. I used to wonder if I'd ever to get to see snow close up.

(smiles dreamily)

Ah, the South, it seems so far away.

(sings softly)

I wish I was in the Land of Cotton
Old times there are not forgotten.

(louder, then motions for others to join in)

ALL   *Look away! Look away! Look away, Dixie Land.*

In Dixie Land where I was born-in
Early on one frosty morn-in
Look away! Look away! Look away, Dixie Land.

I wish I was in Dixie. Hoo-Ray. Hoo-Ray!
In Dixie Land I'll take my stand
To live and die in Dixie.

Away, Away, Away down South in Dixie.
Away, Away, Away down South in Dixie.

(repeat)

If They Can Send a Man To the Moon

Characters:	Jim
	Bess
	Lisa
	Don
Setting:	The living room at Chelsea Cove Retirement Home
Props:	None

....

JIM   I didn't sleep very well last night.

BESS   Why not? Didn't you feel well?

JIM   I'm OK. It's my new pillow. It's awful.

BESS   What's wrong with it?

JIM   When I put my head in the middle of it, both sides snap around my ears like a Mae West life preserver. I'm afraid if I roll over, it might smother me.

BESS   I once had a foam rubber pillow that would spring up and bend my neck to a right angle from my body. That wasn't very comfortable either.

JIM   I'd rather sleep on a pair of sneakers.

LISA   My last new pillow had feathers. Not fluffy feathers, but little scratchy things kept wiggling out through the ticking.

DON   Those were chopped up quills, not feathers.

LISA   Well, if the label had said feathers and quills, I wouldn't have bought it.

DON   So you've gone back to your old pillow, haven't you?

LISA   *(laughs)*

How did you guess?

DON   Well, I had a terrific new pillow. I loved it.

BESS   Loved? You don't love it now?

DON   No. Within a couple of weeks, the fluffy stuff inside packed down into a hard lump. I'm back with my old one, too.

LISA   Lots of things we buy aren't what they are supposed to be.

JIM   True! Did anybody notice those khaki trousers I wore last week? Well, they fit fine until they were washed. Now they're more like walking shorts.

BESS   They shrunk?

JIM   They sure did. And the label said they were washable.

BESS   Fabric that shrinks is as bad as elastic that gives way. So many waistbands look great until the elastic quits.

LISA   Quality isn't what it used to be. It seems that almost everything I buy has to go back to the store at least once. Just recently, my brand new clock wouldn't ring, so I returned it.

DON   You're lucky they took it back. Some stores won't.

JIM   What about that little catch on warranties? A thing may be guaranteed for ninety days, but you have to have the original box to return it.

DON   Who keeps a box for three months?

LISA   Who has the space to keep empty boxes?

BESS   My favorite peeve is buying something sealed in a plastic bubble over cardboard. It looks OK, but you can't check the merchandise until you buy it.

JIM   And if you open the shrink-wrapped plastic package, the store refuses to take it back.

LISA	While we're at it, let's talk about service! I took my car in for a squeaking noise. They sold me four new tires, but it still squeaked.
DON	What did you do next?
LISA	I took it back and they said maybe I needed a brake job.
DON	Just maybe? What about the new tires, did you keep them?
LISA	Sure. So now, I've got new brakes and new tires and it still squeaks.
JIM	Well, if the tires and the brakes aren't the problem, what is?
LISA	They said they'll have to pull the gas tank and check the fuel pump.
DON	For more money?
LISA	Of course!
JIM	Did you mention that they had already sold you tires and brakes?
LISA	Sure. But they said they explained that those were only possibilities.
DON	Am I surprised to hear that?
BESS	How about airline reservations? I made reservations for a trip three weeks in advance and when I got to the airport, they put me on standby.
LISA	Standby! Why?
BESS	They overbooked.
JIM	Do we sound like four grumpy people, or what?
BESS	You could answer your question. Did you sleep well on your new pillow?
LISA	And can you wear your new khaki trousers?

DON   Well, it seems to me if they can send a man to the moon, we should be able to demand high quality products and service.

JIM   Maybe the moon is where things are being made!

BESS   *(laughs)*

               Maybe not the moon, but nothing is made in this country any more.

LISA   I bought an American flag to give my grandson for his birthday. Would you like to guess where it was made?

JIM   On the moon?

LISA   Close enough. Let's go to lunch.

It's Not Nice To Fool Mother Nature

Characters:	Noreen
	Velta
	Ray
Setting:	The television room at Medford Manor, a senior residence
Props:	None

. . . .

RAY   *(points to TV)*

Is this a rerun of an old show?

NOREEN   No, in fact, it's coming live from Carnegie Hall.

RAY   But that's Mimi Maurice! She looks exactly like she did forty years ago.

NOREEN   Yes, isn't science wonderful?

VELTA   Meow!

RAY   What d'ya mean science?

NOREEN   For starters, look at her hair. There isn't a gray one on her head.

VELTA   *(touches her own hair)*

Well, I always say if a woman wasn't supposed to change her hair, then why were all those little bottles of color invented?

NOREEN   Oh, you know what I mean, Velta.

RAY   Forget the red hair. So what if it's colored? Just look at her face! And that figure! She's still gorgeous.

NOREEN   Sure, she is. More science.

VELTA   Oh, come on Noreen! Surely, you can't object if a woman gets a little help when she needs it.

RAY   She doesn't look like she needs any help to me!

VELTA   That proves my point.

RAY   *(leans toward the TV)*

I saw Mimi do a U.S.O. show when I was in the army. She sang that exact same song, and still dances like she always did.

NOREEN   Well, I think we should just accept ourselves the way nature made us.

RAY   Girls! Girls! Enough! Let's try to hear the rest of the song.

NOREEN   Say what you will, Velta. But you can't expect all of us to run out and get all the work done that Mimi Maurice has had.

VELTA   Of course not. But all of us aren't in the public eye.

RAY   Come on ladies. Just watch Mimi dance, won't you?

NOREEN   Humph! Anybody could dance if they worked out every day like some of those actresses do.

VELTA   Then sign me up for a workout class!

RAY   Me too. I wanna keep what I've got left.

NOREEN   You two are hopeless! There's nothing wrong with aging. It's a natural thing. You're acting like it's shameful.

VELTA   Nonsense, Noreen. Is a broken tooth shameful?

NOREEN   No, of course not.

VELTA   So, should a person just accept it and not have it fixed?

NOREEN   It's not the same thing. Ray, tell Velta that Mimi Maurice gets work done strictly out of vanity.

RAY   Probably. But I shave every day for vanity and no-
                 body cares. And I have shoulder pads in my jacket.
                 So what?

NOREEN   Well! Don't you remember that TV slogan that said
                 "It's not nice to fool Mother Nature"?

RAY   That was a margarine commercial, Noreen!

VELTA   *(points to her own lip)*

                 Oh, Noreen, I think your lipstick is smeared.
                 Right there at the corner.

NOREEN   Don't be smart, Velta. You know what I mean.

                 (storms offstage)

                 Mimi Maurice indeed!

Molly Was the One

Note to Activity Director: Before this skit is performed, photocopy the lyrics (page 128) and pass them out to all participants.

Characters:	Henry
	Del
	Charlie
	Art (Pick the best singer in the group to be Art)
Setting:	Four men are at a card table
Prop:	A wallet stuffed with green paper

. . . .

HENRY　　*(makes a grand show of thumbing through the "money")*

I can't believe I got another royal flush! I hate to brag, boys, but some nights Old Henry just can't get a bad hand.

DEL　　*(glumly)*

Well, maybe Old Henry should learn to win with a little less gloating.

HENRY　　Aw, come on, Del. Don't be a sore loser. You'll win some time.

CHARLIE　　Del's right, Henry. We don't mind losing, we just don't like to have our noses rubbed in it.

ART　　Let's not argue, boys. It's still early. We'll just play another hand.

DEL　　Sure, we'll play another hand! Whose deal is it?

HENRY　　Not tonight, boys. Old Henry here is taking his beautiful winnings home.

ART　　But it's not even eleven o'clock, Henry. We never stop before midnight.

CHARLIE	Yeah. Last week I let you guys have a chance to win your money back when I was winning. And it was almost midnight when we started the last game.
HENRY	I'd love to help you out. But I promised the wife I'd get home early.
DEL	Didn't she want you home early last week when Charlie was winning?
ART	Or the week before that when I was winning?
HENRY	She's a little under the weather, so I promised her I wouldn't stay late.
DEL	My wife is pretty understanding about the time I get home.

(looks at Art)

	But, I guess you've never had wife worries, have you, Art? You being a bachelor and all.
ART	Nope. Can't say I have.
CHARLIE	Which reminds me, Artie. My wife's sister is coming for two weeks next Friday. Abbie thought you might like to come for dinner and meet her.
HENRY	Hey, there you go, Art! You'll get a home cooked meal and a chance to meet the sister-in-law, too.
ART	That's real nice of you and Abbie, Charlie. But I don't think I'll come.
DEL	Why not, Art? If the sister looks anything like Charlie's wife, you'd be lucky to have dinner with her.
ART	I just don't want to get involved with any lady.
CHARLIE	Is that how you stayed single all these years, Artie? By avoiding women?
HENRY	Yeah, Art. All you do is play poker with the guys and you never even have a date. What fun is that?

ART	Stop it, you guys. I'll do what I want to do.
DEL	They're right, Art. Don't be a stick in the mud. I've always spent time with a lot of ladies. *(laughs)* My wives didn't like it, but I had fun!
ART	Well, Del, you're the other extreme. Me, I just know that no woman could ever compare to my first love.
CHARLIE	You had a first love?! You never mentioned her.
DEL	This is a shocker! Tell us about her, Art.
HENRY	Yeah, tell us about her. But make it quick. I've gotta be getting home.
ART	OK. It was a long time ago. She was a sweet and gentle girl.
CHARLIE	She must have really been something, to make you swear off girls forever, Artie. What was her name?
ART	Molly.
DEL	Where did you know her from?
ART	It was back in the old country. When I wasn't much more than a kid myself. *(begins singing)* *In Dublin's fair city, where girls are so pretty.* *I first set my eyes on sweet Molly Malone.* *(the other three join the singing)* *As she pushed her wheel barrow* *Through streets broad and narrow* *Crying cockles and mussels alive, alive, oh.* *(the actors motion for everybody in the room to join the singing)*
ALL	*Alive, alive, oh. Alive, alive, oh.* *Crying cockles and mussels alive, alive, oh.*

She was a fishmonger, but sure 'twas no wonder,
For so were her father and mother before,
And they each pushed their wheelbarrow
Through streets broad and narrow.

Crying cockles and mussels alive, alive, oh!
Alive, alive, oh,
Alive, alive, oh.
Crying cockles and mussels alive, alive, oh.

CHARLIE   Well, why on earth didn't you marry the girl, Art
old boy? Why'd you let her get away?

ALL   *She died of a 'faver and no one could save her,*
And that was the end of sweet Molly Malone.
Her ghost wheels her barrow
Through streets broad and narrow
Crying cockles and mussels alive, alive, oh!

Alive, alive, oh,
Alive, alive, oh,
Crying cockles and mussels alive, alive, oh.

HENRY   *(pats Art on the shoulder, then pats his wallet)*

And I'll be going now. Good night fellas.

Cockles and Mussels

In Dublin's fair city, where girls are so pretty,
I first set my eyes on sweet Molly Malone.
As she pushed her wheellbarrow,
Through streets broad and narrow,
Crying cockles and mussels alive, alive, oh!
Alive, alive, oh,
Alive, alive, oh,
Crying cockles and mussels alive, alive, oh!

She was a fishmonger, but sure 'twas no wonder,
For so were her father and mother before.
And they each pushed their wheelbarrow,
Through streets broad and narrow,
Crying cockles and mussels alive, alive, oh!
Alive, alive, oh,
Alive, alive, oh,
Crying cockles and mussels alive, alive, oh!

She died of a 'faver and no one could save her,
And that was the end of sweet Molly Malone.
Her ghost wheels her barrow,
Through streets broad and narrow,
Crying cockles and mussels alive, alive, oh!
Alive, alive, oh,
Alive, alive, oh,
Crying cockles and mussels alive, alive, oh!

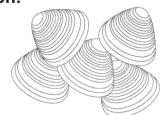

Off To the Races

Characters: Merrill (a woman or a man)
               Pat (a woman or a man)

Setting: A window at Willow Grove Senior Home

Props: None

. . . .

MERRILL   Hello, Pat. Beautiful morning, isn't it?

PAT   Hi Merrill. It sure is. I can't think of a nicer
               day to be going to the races.

MERRILL   You're going to the races? So am I. Maybe I'll see
               you there.

PAT   I'd like that. Do you have a favorite horse?

MERRILL   Not really. I just read the racing form when I get
               there and then I decide if I want to place a bet.

PAT   That's the way I do it. Sometimes I win a little,
               but not usually.

MERRILL   Me too. I just allow myself so much to play with.
               And if I win a race, then I'll have more to play
               with than I planned on. That's always fun.

PAT   Have you ever won a longshot?

MERRILL   I sure have. Then I bet it all on the very next
               longshot and lost it all.

PAT   The betting isn't really why I go. I just enjoy
               watching the horses. They're so beautiful.

MERRILL   I admire the jockeys. It takes a lot of courage to
               race along on a horse when all those thundering
               hooves are all around you.

PAT   I know. Jockeys aren't very big, but every pound
               of them is pure athlete. They have to be strong to
               control an animal that size.

MERRILL   All this talk about racing is making me want to
               get going. See you there.

PAT   Right. See you at the track.

               (walks away humming Camptown Races)

               *(both Pat and Merrill turn and invite the group to join in
               singing)*

ALL   *Camptown Ladies sing this song, Doo Dah! Doo Dah!*
               Camptown Race Track's five miles long,
               Oh, Doo Dah Day!
               Goin' to run all night, goin' to run all day,
               Bet my money on a bobtail nag,
               Somebody bet on the bay.

Old Smokey

Characters: Bonnie Lou
             Marty

Setting: The social room of the retirement center.

Props: None

. . . .

MARTY   Hello there, Ma'am. You're new here, aren't you?
                My name is Marty.

                (sticks out hand)

BONNIE LOU *(shakes his hand)*

                Hello, Marty. Yes, I just moved in. I'm Bonnie Lou.

MARTY   Welcome! I hope you'll feel right at home here.

BONNIE LOU *(sighs)*

                I hope so. It's certainly a big change for me.

MARTY   You'll do just fine, Bonnie Lou. The people are
                all very nice. It took me a little while, but I've
                come to feel like this is my home now.

BONNIE LOU Oh? Where did you come from?

MARTY   I'm from Maine originally. Grew up on the coast.
                So you see, this is quite different from what I
                was used to. Where are you from?

BONNIE LOU Far from Maine! I came from a little farm in the
                Great Smokey Mountains. This is definitely not
                what I'm used to.

MARTY   Most of us are from somewhere else. But not count-
                ing mealtime, there's one thing that brings us all
                together.

BONNIE LOU What's that?

MARTY It's our sing-alongs.

BONNIE LOU You have sing-alongs?! Wonderful! I'm going to enjoy that.

MARTY There's one song we always sing that is everybody's favorite. It should make you feel right at home.

BONNIE LOU Really? I'll bet I know what it is!

MARTY I'll bet you do.

(smiles, starts to sing, and motions all to join in)

ALL *On top of Old Smokey, all covered with snow,*
I lost my true lover, for courtin' too slow.

For courting's a pleasure, and parting is grief,
And a false-hearted lover is worse than a thief.

For a thief will just rob you, and take what you have,
But a false-hearted lover, will lead you to the grave.

They'll hug you and kiss you, and tell you more lies,
Than cross-ties on a railroad or stars in the skies.

Come all you young maidens, and listen to me,
Never place your affections, on a green willow tree.

For the leaves they will wither, the roots will all die.
You'll all be forsaken, and never know why.

(repeat)

Telling Time

Characters: Maggie
                  Mike

Setting: The solarium at Brookfield Senior Residence

Prop: A watch

. . . .

MIKE   *(puts his watch to his ear)*

Maggie, what time is it? I think my watch is running slow.

MAGGIE   I don't know. I left mine on my dresser.

MIKE   There's a clock on the wall behind the bookcase, but the face is too small to read it from here.

MAGGIE   It only has dots where the numbers should be. So I can't be sure.

MIKE   *(laughs)*

Should we go outside and look at the sundial in the garden?

MAGGIE   Not a bad idea. But I'm not concerned because I'm going anywhere.

MIKE   And when it's time to eat, we'll see people heading toward the dining room.

MAGGIE   So, who needs a watch?

MIKE   *(taps his watch)*

I probably just need a new battery.

MAGGIE   I used to love the old fashioned clocks that were popular when I was a girl.

MIKE	What kind of clock was that, Maggie?
MAGGIE	Oh, you know, Grandfather Clocks. They were so tall you could read the time from across the room.
MIKE	My family had one. It was made of carved rosewood with ornate paintings on its face.
MAGGIE	We had one made of mahogany. It rang on the hour and the half hour. Beautiful chimes.
MIKE	Clocks used to be works of art. Do you remember the pocket watches that men used to carry?
MAGGIE	I sure do. My grandpa's had a case that opened and closed. It was yellow gold with a train engine engraved on it in platinum.
MIKE	Where is it today?
MAGGIE	I think my dad's older brother got it, so one of his kids probably has it now.
MIKE	Too bad. That would be an heirloom.
MAGGIE	I know. But I do have my mother's locket watch. It's one of my most treasured possessions.
MIKE	I'd like to see it.
MAGGIE	I'll wear it to dinner tonight. I'd love to show it to you.
MIKE	I'd feel lost without my watch.
MAGGIE	I used to live by the clock. Everything was rush, rush, rush.
MIKE	Me too. I always had a plane to catch or a meeting to get to.
MAGGIE	It's so much more relaxing now without rushing around.
MIKE	Yeah, we've earned the luxury of setting our own schedules.

MAGGIE   I know. Maybe I'll just go sit on the porch and watch people hurrying down the road in their cars.

MIKE   That's a fine idea. Mind if I join you?

MAGGIE   Not at all. We've earned the leisure.

MIKE   You've got a good point there.

                  (touches his wrist watch)

                  Y'know? Maybe I need a battery, maybe not. I'll get around to buying one when I have the time.

                  (both laugh)

The Skies Are Not Cloudy

Characters: Eleanora
             Roger
             Carrie

Setting: Breakfast Room

Prop: Magazine

. . . .

ELEANORA *(holds magazine)*

Did you guys see this latest issue of Ideal Home?

CARRIE Not yet. But I like the magazine because it has articles on all kinds of homes. Mobile homes, apartments, duplexes.

ROGER You mean it doesn't just cover articles on big private estates?

ELEANORA Oh, no! This issue has a lot of hints about apartment living that we could use right here.

CARRIE Anything about storage? I never have enough closet and storage space.

ELEANORA Actually, it does. I'll lend it to both of you when I'm through with it.

ROGER Thanks, but I'll pass.

ELEANORA Why, Roger? Is your place exactly the way you want it to be?

ROGER *(shrugs)*

It's OK.

ELEANORA Just OK? Then I'll bet there are still a few changes you could make. There's always room for improvement.

ROGER   Oh, probably. But I'll tell you the home that I'd
             really like.

CARRIE   What would you like, Roger?

ROGER   *(grins, starts singing, and motions all to join)*

ALL   *Oh, give me a home, where the buffalo roam,*
             Where the deer and the antelope play.
             Where seldom is heard a discouraging word,
             And the skies are not cloudy all day.

             Home, home on the range,
             Where the deer and the antelope play.
             Where seldom is heard a discouraging word,
             And the skies are not cloudy all day.

Section 6

Nostalgia and Reminiscence

Daisy

Characters: Charlene
              Steve
              Mark

Setting: Activity Room at the Heather Hill Retirement Home

Props: None

. . . .

CHARLENE   *(speaks slowly, as if deep in thought)*

               Heather Hill Retirement Home. How do you suppose
               this place got its name?

STEVE   I don't know. Heather Hill sounds like a lady's
               name to me.

MARK   I think it sounds like a mountain covered with
               flowers.

CHARLENE   Maybe it was named for an actual lady who happened
               to be named for a mountain covered with flowers.

STEVE   Possibly. As a matter of fact, I've known several
               ladies named Heather.

MARK   Were they actually named for flowers?

STEVE   Not that they mentioned.

MARK   Were any of them married to a guy named Hill?

STEVE   Not that I know of. In fact, a couple of them
               never married at all.

CHARLENE   Since we're on the subject, have any of you ever
               seen any heather growing around here? I've seen
               lots of other kinds of flowers, but no heather.

STEVE   I haven't seen any either...just roses. Every
               house in the entire county has at least one rose

bush. Some have dozens. Maybe they should have named it Rose Hill Retirement Home.

MARK   I've seen lots of Black-Eyed-Susans growing wild along the roads. They could have called it Black-Eyed-Susan Hill.

CHARLENE   I heard that the Black-Eyed-Susan is in the daisy family.

MARK   I like the name Daisy. It has an old-fashioned ring to it.

STEVE   Yes, Daisy's a nice name. Reminds me of the Boy Scouts.

MARK   A Daisy reminds you of the Boy Scouts? If there had been a scout named Daisy in our troop, we'd have sent him home.

STEVE   No, of course none of the scouts were named Daisy.

MARK   Then why does Daisy remind you of the scouts?

STEVE   Well, when I was a scout, we went camping. And we sat around campfires in the evening. And, what do scouts do when they're sitting around a campfire?

CHARLENE   They eat hot dogs and marshmallows?

STEVE   Well, yes, they do that. But what else do they do?

CHARLENE   They tell ghost stories and try to frighten each other so they can't sleep?

STEVE   Yeah, I guess they do that too. But what else do they do around a campfire?

CHARLENE   They talk about their mothers?

STEVE   No.

CHARLENE   They talk about girls?

STEVE   Well, sometimes, maybe. But what else do they do?

MARK   They sing campfire songs?

STEVE   There you go!

CHARLENE   Now, I get the connection! Was "Daisy" one of the
                 songs you sang?

STEVE   Right! And here is how it goes.

                 (motions everybody to join in the song)

ALL   *Daisy, Daisy. Give me your answer, do!*
                 I'm half crazy, all for the love of you.
                 It won't be a stylish marriage.
                 I can't afford a carriage.
                 But you'll look sweet, upon the seat
                 Of a bicycle built for two.

                 (repeat)

Down in the Valley

Characters:	Jeb
	Emma
	Johnny

Setting: A cottage somewhere down south

Props: Three chairs, a table, a cup, a paper bag

· ·

JEB   *(answers a knock from an imaginary door)*

Howdy, stranger. What brings you to our house so
early in the mornin'?

JOHNNY   I seen the smoke from your chimney. Could you
spare a cup of coffee?

JEB   Why sure, young man. Come in. Emma jest finished
perkin' a fresh pot. Sit yourself down right there.

(points to chair)

EMMA   *(hands him a cup of coffee)*

Here you go. Do you take milk or sugar in it?

JOHNNY   *(sits down)*

Thank you kindly, ma'am. Plain is fine.

(takes a sip)

This coffee tastes real good. I was gettin' mighty
dry without a thing to drink all night.

JEB   If you don't mind my sayin' so, young feller, you
look plumb tuckered out.

(takes a sip)

Do you live around these parts?

JOHNNY	No.
	(sighs heavily)
	No, my home is far from here.
EMMA	Then where did you sleep last night? Have you been walkin' these hills all night long?
	(takes a sip)
JOHNNY	I'm afraid so, ma'am.
	(shakes his head)
	And more time than not, I was runnin'.
	(takes a sip)
JEB	You was runnin' these hills after dark? Runnin' from what?
JOHNNY	Never mind that, sir. I'll just finish up this coffee and be on my way. I really do appreciate your kindness.
	(takes a sip)
	I'd better hurry along.
EMMA	*(raises her hand to stop him)*
	No need to rush right out, boy. What's your name?
	(fixes food and puts it in a bag)
JOHNNY	Johnny.
EMMA	Well, Johnny, you're not much older than my youngest boy. And I won't let you leave this house without seein' you get a proper bite to eat. Here, take this.
	(hands him the bag)
	It's not much, just some bread and meat.

JOHNNY   Bless you, ma'am. You don't know how much I'll appreciate eating this.

JEB   Whatever the problem is, boy, runnin' ain't the answer. Maybe if you jest stop and catch your breath, you can face it in the light of day.

JOHNNY   I wish it was that simple. Now look, you folks have been good to me. But I really have to go before you get in trouble from helping me out.

EMMA   Sounds like you're the one who's in trouble, Johnny. Why not wait here with us and we'll see if we can help you find a way to solve it.

JOHNNY   I wish you could. But it's too late for that.

JEB   Johnny, you seem like a nice young feller. If there's anything we can do...

(shakes his head sadly and begins to sing, motioning everybody to join in)

ALL   *Down in the valley, valley so low.*
Hang your head over, hear the wind blow.
Hear the wind blow, dear, hear the wind blow.
Hang your head over, hear the wind blow.

Roses love sunshine, violets love dew.
Angels in heaven know I love you.
Know I love you, dear, know I love you.
Angels in heaven know I love you.

Write me a letter, send it by mail.
Send it care of the Birmingham Jail.
Birmingham Jail, dear, Birmingham Jail.
Send it in care of the Birmingham Jail.

Down in the valley, valley so low.
Hang your head over, hear the wind blow.
Hear the wind blow, dear, hear the wind blow.
Hang your head over, hear the wind blow.

JOHNNY   *(as song ends, he grabs the bag and hurries out)*

Thank you kindly.

For Me and My Gal

Characters: Paul
               Ann
               Lori

Setting: The breakfast table at Eastbrook Senior Residence

Props: Table, three chairs

. . . .

PAUL   Morning, ladies. May I join you?

ANN   Hello, Paul. Sure, have a seat.

               (gestures to a chair)

LORI   Hi, Paul. You're looking bright today. Any particular reason?

PAUL   I saw a rerun of "For Me And My Gal" last night and I'm still humming.

LORI   Judy Garland and Gene Kelly! Those two were so great together they could have made a statue smile.

ANN   What is it about musicals that makes everybody happy? Is it the music? The dancing?

PAUL   Both of those?

LORI   Maybe it's the plot. Musicals are usually love stories. And everybody loves romance.

ANN   Maybe it's just the innocence of the musicals. Simple stories and songs that lift you up and get your feet tapping.

LORI   It's all of those things. Who can feel bad when they're watching a love story?

ANN   Here it is 50 or 60 years after they made that
                   movie, and we're still singing the songs from it.
                   I think that's the mark of a great show...that
                   it's remembered years later.

PAUL   And there were so many good songs in it. There was
                   "When You Wore a Tulip."

LORI   And "Over There."

PAUL   And "Long, Long Trail."

ANN   I loved the costumes. The women looked so feminine
                   in those dresses and hats.

LORI   Well, I liked Gene Kelly's smile. Tap dancing is a
                   lot of work, but he made it look so easy with that
                   big smile on his face.

ANN   Wasn't he a bad guy in that movie?

PAUL   He was sort of a bad, but with a heart of gold.
                   You know the type.

                   (points to his own chest)

LORI   Yes, we know the type, Paul.

                   (looks at him teasingly)

                   But you're not really too bad.

ANN   *(studies Paul's face)*

                   And maybe you do look a little like Gene Kelly
                   from the side angle.

LORI   The question is, can you tap dance?

PAUL   *(laughs)*

                   I stick with the two-step these days.

ANN   Well, can you sing?

PAUL   *(starts singing, motions for all to join in)*

ALL
*The bells are ringing for me and my gal.
The birds are singing for me and my gal.
Everybody's been knowing
To a wedding they're going
And for weeks they've been sewing
Every Susie and Sal.*

*They're congregating for me and my gal.
The Parson's waiting for me and my gal.
And sometime soon
I'm goin' to build a little home for two,
Or three or four or more
In Love Land for me and my gal.*

*What a beautiful day, for a wedding in May.
See the people all stare, at the lovable pair.*

*She's a vision of joy, he's the luckiest boy.
In his wedding array hear him smilingly say*

(repeat)

How Ya Gonna Keep 'Em Down On the Farm?

Characters: Pa
                Ma
                Orville
                Buck
                Lula Belle

Setting: The front porch of the old farmhouse

Props: A big wad of green paper (money) and a cardboard tube
                (shotgun)

• •

PA   Orville! Buck! What tuck you so long getting'
home? Where you been?

MA   We been settin' here waitin' for you. It's after
midnight. I needed them provisions I sent you fer,
fer our supper.

LULA BELLE Yeah, where you been? Pa, take 'em to the wood
shed and thrash 'em.

BUCK   Shut your fly trap, Lula Belle. Maybe I'll tell
what time Clem brung you home last night.

ORVILLE   *(points to chest)*

No need to worry about us, Ma. We're all growed up.

BUCK   *(snorts)*

Besides, what could happen to us between town and
home? We been down that road a million times.

MA   Well, fer starters, you coulda run that truck off
the road into the river and drowneded.

ORVILLE   You know we both swim like greased water moccasins,
Ma.

BUCK   Yeah, we been swimmin' ever since we was knee-high
to a tadpole.

ORVILLE   Besides, dunkin' that old truck in the river might be a good idea. Then Pa could collect on the IN-surance policy and git his-self a new truck.

MA   You boys know yer Pa don't have no IN-surance.

PA   If you boys ever dunk my truck, you're a-buyin' me a new one.

LULA BELLE What with, Pa? Their good looks? Or should I say, what they wished was their good looks?

MA   I worried that you two done got yer pockets picked by some city slicker.

BUCK   *(pats pocket)*

                Oh, Ma. Ain't no city slicker big enough to pick our pockets. Orville and me's the biggest dudes in the county.

LULA BELLE The biggest dunces, you mean. They're jest not smart like my Clem, Pa.

PA   You still ain't said where you been all night, boys.

ORVILLE   You know the Blue Moon Saloon? Well it was the durndest thing, Pa. Your truck done run out of gas right in front of it.

BUCK   So we went inside to find out where was the nearest filling station.

ORVILLE   And the purtiest lady you ever seed come up and started a-dancin' and a-gyratin' right in front of us. She said her friend was startin' a card game at a table and asked us to set in on it.

BUCK   So we figured jest one hand of poker wouldn't hurt nothin'.

MA   But Orville, them's the kind of wimmen I told you to stay away from!

LULA BELLE I bet them wimmen was all painted up purty, wasn't they?

(shakes her head in disgust)

Boy, are you two dumb.

ORVILLE   Shut your pie cabinet, Lula Belle.

PA   So you set down for jest one game?

(snorts)

And did them wimmen blow on your cards for luck?

ORVILLE   Well, yeah.

LULA BELLE   Oh, Man! You two got no sense, not like my Clem. He's savin' his money so's we can get married. He must have two or three hundred dollars by now.

ORVILLE   Well, Lula Belle. So long as yer comparing us to Clem, I want you to take a gander at this.

(pulls a wad of green paper from pocket)

Buck and me jest happened to win every cent old Clem had on him.

LULA BELLE   What??? You won all that money from my Clem? At the Blue Moon Saloon? But he's a travelin' man. And he's travelin' this week to make money for us to get married on.

ORVILLE   Ha! He durn sure traveled to the Blue Moon Saloon.

BUCK   Double Ha!

PA   Lula Belle, I don't trust that man Clem. Maybe he jest lost all his money to get outta marryin' you.

MA   Leave the girl be, Pa. You'll hurt her feelins. She can't help it she's sixteen and still not married.

LULA BELLE   But I was a-gonna GIT married!

PA   And yer STILL gonna git married. Even a travelin' man is better than no man at all.

ORVILLE   Well, I'll bet by tomorrow that travelin' man will have traveled. He'll be long gone.

PA   *(picks up his shotgun)*

Nope. Boys, you and me's going back to the Blue Moon Saloon tonight. We're gonna make real sure that travelin' man don't do no travelin'. Not 'til he's hitched up with my Lula Belle.

(the men walk away, leaving Ma and Lula Belle)

MA   *(puts arm around Lula Belle)*

Lula Belle, honey, all this excitement takes me back to when your Pa and me was a-courtin'.

(smiles)

Ain't love grand?

Lazy Hazy Days

Characters: Ralph
Lottie

Setting: The old fishing hole, on a hot, muggy afternoon

Props: A fishing pole (a stick with string attached), a bucket (for imaginary worms), a bottle

. . . .

RALPH   Ain't this a nice day for fishin', Lottie?

LOTTIE   Sure is, Ralph. It was a right smart idea you had to bring these foldin' chairs, too. Jest look at you. Yer settin' right smack in the water.

RALPH   Sure feels good, Babe. Say, can you bring me my fishin' pole from the shore yonder?

LOTTIE   *(wades in and gives him the pole)*

Here you go, Ralph.

(wades back and sits down)

RALPH   Say, Lottie. Do you think you could get me a cold one from that cooler in the back of the truck?

LOTTIE   *(gets up and goes to side stage, then wades to him with bottle)*

Here you are, Ralphie. My, you sure do look comfortable settin' there like that.

RALPH   This is the life, I'll tell you.

(pauses)

Um, Sweetie, would you do me a favor and get that bucket o' night crawlers from over yonder?

(points to a tree)

LOTTIE   *(sighs)*

Why, sure, Ralph.

(wades to him with bucket)

RALPH   Thanks, Lottie. While yer here, will you put a nice fat one of the end of my hook for me?

LOTTIE   Aw, come on, Ralph. You know I hate touchin' them things.

RALPH   But Lottie, honey, I'm a-holdin' my bottle so my hands ain't free.

LOTTIE   Well, caint you put it down?

RALPH   Where? In the water? It would spill for sure. Come on, Lottie, put jest one nice fat worm on my hook.

LOTTIE   Oh, all right.

(winces and puts imaginary worm on hook)

RALPH   Ain't this the life, Lottie?

LOTTIE   *(shakes her hands in disgust)*

Now look at my fingers. They're all wet and gooey from baitin' that hook.

RALPH   Well yer in the water. Jest wash 'em off.

LOTTIE   *(pretends to wash hands)*

I'm goin' to move right over under that tree. I'd hate to scare the fish away from you.

RALPH   Don't move, Lottie. I've got a bite.

(hands her the stick)

Here, Honey. Give him a little slack on the line so he'll get tired.

LOTTIE   But I ain't fishin', Ralph. You are.

RALPH I told you my hands was full with this bottle. Now you give me a little help.

LOTTIE Oh, all right.

(moves stick around)

Look, Ralph. He's a real fighter.

RALPH Give him room to run, Lottie! Then reel him in nice and slow.

LOTTIE He's a beauty, Ralph. And he's a strong one.

RALPH Easy now, Lottie. Reel him nice and easy. You don't wanna lose him.

LOTTIE *(moves slowly back and forth, reeling)*

Look at the size of him! He's tiring me out!

RALPH Well, jest keep it up, Lottie. Soon as you bring him in, you can clean him and start a fire over there by the truck. Now take it easy on that reel.

LOTTIE OK, OK. I think he's about done for. I'll have him in a minute.

RALPH *(leans back in his chair)*

Fishin' is about the best thing a man can do.

LOTTIE No kiddin'?

RALPH Yep. Nothin' like a day of fishin' to relax a man.

LOTTIE *(hands him the stick)*

You said a mouthful, Ralph.

Little Brown Jug

Characters: Billy Ray
Clem

Setting: In the shade of a tree

Props: None

．．

CLEM Do I recollect right, or is yours and Milly Lou's anniversary comin' up?

BILLY RAY Yep. It sure is. It's gonna be a whole year next week that we been married.

CLEM A whole year! Seems like yesterday. Didn't that time go fast?

BILLY RAY It sure did.

CLEM I could tell from the start that the two of you was made for each other.

BILLY RAY That's what I thought when I first saw her standin' in the store where she worked with the neon State Lottery sign flashin' over her head.

CLEM That's bee-yo-tee-ful, Billy Ray. There ain't nothin' like true love to bind a marriage together.

BILLY RAY I know it. And there won't ever be another woman for me.

CLEM I'm gettin' all choked up, Billy Ray.

BILLY RAY Still and all, I don't think that Milly Lou is happy.

CLEM Lordy, Billy Ray! Milly Lou sure seems happy to me.

BILLY RAY Well, she puts on a good face. But I don't think she's truly happy.

CLEM   I hate to ask, Billy Ray, but she ain't got eyes for nobody else, has she?

BILLY RAY   Naw! Course not! It's jest that she's a jealous woman, Clem.

CLEM   If yer straight and true, like you say, what's she got to be jealous of?

BILLY RAY   She's jealous of jest about everything I like, if it ain't her.

CLEM   Like what?

BILLY RAY   Well, for one thing, she's jealous of time I spend with my old hound dog, Blue.

CLEM   Maybe she's afraid you'll get fleas.

BILLY RAY   Naw, I've got flea soap for that.

CLEM   Then what else is there?

BILLY RAY   She's jealous of the time I spend under the hood of my truck fixin' it, too.

CLEM   A man's gotta fix his truck.

BILLY RAY   I know it. And she knows it, too. But she don't like it anyway.

CLEM   Oh, you know wimmen. They don't mean it when they're jealous.

BILLY RAY   Maybe. But there's one more thing that makes her turn wild.

CLEM   What's that, Billy Ray?

BILLY RAY   She even hates my little brown jug.

CLEM   *(shakes head sadly)*

I guess wimmen can be pretty unreasonable.

(both begin singing)

My wife and I live all alone, in a little brown
hut we call our own.
I love her and she loves me.
But the little brown jug, how I love thee.
Ha ha ha. You and me.
Little brown jug how I love thee.

Ha ha ha. You and me.
Little brown jug how I love thee.

(repeat)

Sailing With Columbus

Characters: King Ferdinand
               Queen Isabella I
               Christopher Columbus

Setting: The Royal Court of Spain late in the fifteenth century

Prop: An apple

. . . .

KING   Señor Columbus, how can Her Majesty and myself be sure that you have had enough experience to do the job you want to do?

COLUMBUS   Well, sir, I was born in the seaport of Genoa, Italy. For a time I plied my father's trade of weaving, but have sailed since my twenties.

QUEEN   *(scoffs)*

               You have sailed? As a passenger? A galley hand? As what?

COLUMBUS   I have commanded ships for many years, Your Majesty.

QUEEN   Can I assume that means you have never lost a ship?

COLUMBUS   Regretfully, that is not the case, Madam.

KING   Aha! You have lost a ship? Under what circumstances?

COLUMBUS   Sixteen years ago I was in a convoy bound for England. Pirates attacked and sank my ship off the coast of Portugal.

QUEEN   Pirates? And you lived to tell the tale? What happened?

COLUMBUS   I swam to shore, Your Majesty.

QUEEN   You swam as your ship went down? You swam past pirates?

COLUMBUS   Yes, Your Grace. With great struggle I reached the shores of Lisbon.

KING   I don't know why I believe your tall tale, but I do. But tell me, why would a man go back to sea after such a frightening misadventure?

COLUMBUS   The sea is in my blood, my King.

KING   All right. Let's move on. As you spin your tales, explain again about this strange idea you have.

COLUMBUS   Well, sir. I believe the earth is round. And I intend to prove it to you.

QUEEN   Round? Ha! But, I suppose we can amuse ourselves by listening to you.

COLUMBUS   Thank you, my Queen. As a sea captain, I have studied many maps. I have watched the sun rise and set. I have seen many ships in the distance.

KING   As we all have! What has this to do with the earth being...ha-ha...round?

COLUMBUS   When you watch a ship sail away, what part of it do you see last?

KING   Why, the mast of course.

COLUMBUS   Yes. The very top of the mast. If the earth were flat, you would see the entire ship disappear at once.

KING   *(strokes his chin)*

Hmmmm.

COLUMBUS   *(picks up an apple)*

Look, Your Majesty. This apple is round. If I lift my finger up behind it, you see the tip of my finger first, then the entire hand.

QUEEN *(leans closer)*

The apple is indeed round.

(moves her hand behind it)

Very interesting.

KING One moment, Señor. You are Italian, but married to a Portuguese woman and live in Lisbon. Why are you here at the Royal Court of Spain seeking funding for this wild adventure?

COLUMBUS Because I have heard that you and Queen Isabella are modern thinkers.

QUEEN And...?

COLUMBUS *(smiles broadly)*

And because Portugal turned down my proposal.

QUEEN So Spain is your second choice?

COLUMBUS Finance me, my Queen. Give me ships to sail west to India. I will give Spain a quicker, cheaper trade route.

KING That's what you give us, but what will it do for you?

COLUMBUS If you would give me all the lands that I discover on my journey...

QUEEN Absolutely not! All lands will belong to Spain, Señor Columbus.

COLUMBUS Very well. Then name me viceroy of all the lands that I claim for Spain.

KING *(strokes his chin)*

That seems fair enough.

COLUMBUS And, one-tenth of all precious metals from the lands I discover.

QUEEN   Aha! So you ARE a fortune hunter?

COLUMBUS   Should I demand less? After all, I could bring Spain untold wealth.

KING   Señor, please wait in the outer chamber. Her Majesty and I should like to discuss your plan.

COLUMBUS   *(bows his head)*

Yes, Your Majesty.

(leaves)

KING   So, Isabella, what do you think of this dreamer's plan?

QUEEN   It's possible. But let's not invest too much in it. We have three old ships that are expendable. We could outfit him with a minimum of expense.

KING   And what ships would those be, my dear?

QUEEN   The Santa Maria, the Pinta and the Nina.

KING   *(laughs)*

Yes! Those three old tubs!

QUEEN   If he returns, we will give him what he demands.

KING   *(smiles broadly)*

My dear, inside that beautiful head of yours lives a bandit. I admire that in a ruler.

QUEEN   And you, Ferdinand, are a careful gambler. Shall we bring Señor Columbus back in to give him our decision?

KING   *(nods)*

Yes. This may not change the world, but it should be interesting.

The Perfect Kingdom

Characters: King Arthur
             Queen Guinevere
             Sir Lancelot

Setting: Camelot

Prop: One pair of scissors

. . . .

**KING
ARTHUR**   *(pretends to cut a lock of Guinevere's hair)*

Guinevere, tomorrow I must leave you for a
while. But I will carry this lock of your hair
into battle.

GUINEVERE Why must you go, my king? The castle is cold
while you are away.

**KING
ARTHUR**   A horseman brought a message that Anglo-Saxons
have crossed the channel to invade us. I must
defend Camelot.

GUINEVERE Arthur, you must be tired of war.

**KING
ARTHUR**   I am weary of it, Guinevere. But threats to the
crown must be answered.

GUINEVERE Threats, threats! Why won't they let us live in
peace?

**KING
ARTHUR**   They envy us for our perfect kingdom.

GUINEVERE Is it perfect when its king leaves the queen
alone inside the castle walls?

**KING
ARTHUR**   My counselor, Merlin, warns that destruction
could befall us, Guinevere.

GUINEVERE How can I be certain you will return safely?

KING ARTHUR Three of my best knights will go with my army. Sir Percival is a master at jousting. Sir Galahad's lance is fearsome, and Sir Gawain fights like a lion.

GUINEVERE Will your nephew, Mordred, ride with you to battle, Arthur?

KING ARTHUR No, he stays here. Merlin warned me not to trust Mordred in battle.

GUINEVERE Then you are wise to leave him behind.

KING ARTHUR And I shall leave my best knight, Sir Lancelot, here to protect you.

GUINEVERE But the invaders are to the south of us. I shall be safe here at the castle.

KING ARTHUR I do not wish to frighten you, my dear, but Merlin suspects a danger within these very walls. I fear that Mordred may make an attempt on your life.

GUINEVERE Oh! Must you leave me, Arthur?

KING ARTHUR A king must lead his army. Lancelot will guard you with his life.

GUINEVERE Oh, Arthur, you frighten me when you talk this way. Instead, tell me the sweet words a woman longs to hear.

KING ARTHUR You know my feelings for you, Guinevere.

GUINEVERE Perhaps my mind knows them. But my heart yearns for those sweet words.

KING ARTHUR Must you always ask what I feel for you? Is it not enough to know that I chose you to be my queen?

GUINEVERE *(sadly)*

Yes, my lord.

KING ARTHUR *(looks up at a knock on the door)*

Ah, Lancelot! Come in!

LANCELOT King Arthur, I am at your service. Do we leave for battle now?

KING ARTHUR *(shakes his head)*

No, Lancelot. I am leaving my queen to your care. Guard her with your life.

LANCELOT *(aghast)*

Do I understand you, Your Majesty? Have I spent my life learning the skills of battle only to be left behind when my king goes to fight?

KING ARTHUR *(sternly)*

That is my will, Lancelot!

LANCELOT Sir! I am a knight! You leave me behind to defend a...a...woman!

KING ARTHUR Not a woman, Lancelot...your Queen! Do you question my order?

LANCELOT *(bows in humility)*

Forgive me, my lord. It will be my greatest honor to protect Queen Guinevere...with my very life.

KING ARTHUR So be it! I go now.

(takes Guinevere's hand)

Farewell.

(moves off-stage)

GUINEVERE *(haughtily)*

So, sir, it appears you dislike your queen?

LANCELOT *(bows head)*

Not so, Queen Guinevere. I am not worthy to serve you.

GUINEVERE But you would rather be jousting with the Anglo-Saxons?

LANCELOT If I could fight a dragon for you, my soul would leave my body happily.

GUINEVERE *(jokingly)*

Then you will be disappointed if you cannot die for me?

LANCELOT *(smiles)*

I would rather live long and revel in the glow of your beauty.

GUINEVERE *(teasingly)*

Sir, it seems the stories about you are true.

LANCELOT What stories, Madam?

GUINEVERE That every lady-in-waiting from here to France has heard your flattery.

LANCELOT That may have been true before I came here to serve King Arthur. But since I crossed Camelot's moat, my thoughts are only on my queen.

GUINEVERE *(modestly)*

Lancelot!

LANCELOT I shall stand guard against my senses, Lady.

GUINEVERE *(breathlessly)*

What senses must you guard against, sir?

LANCELOT I must not see your beauty. I must not hear the music of your voice. I must turn from the flower-like scent of your hair.

GUINEVERE You have five senses, Lancelot. You mentioned only three.

LANCELOT *(turns away from her)*

Do not torment me so. I dare not even dream of my other senses when I am so near to you.

GUINEVERE The remaining senses are touch and taste. Can a brave knight fear those?

LANCELOT *(looks at her)*

Ah, yes. I fear touch. Because the thought of your touch reduces me to rubble.

GUINEVERE And taste?

LANCELOT *(presses his hand against his lips)*

To taste...I would be lost forever!

GUINEVERE *(turns away)*

Lancelot! Merlin is right. The danger to Camelot lies within these very walls! I pray I am strong enough to resist it.

LANCELOT *(turns from her)*

And I, my lady.

KING ARTHUR *(voice from off-stage)*

Away we go, Knights of the Round Table! A strong force threatens Camelot!

Tip-Toeing Thru Tulips

Characters: Louie
             Josie

Setting: The sun room

Prop: A bouquet of tulips (real, silk, or paper)

. . . .

JOSIE   Louie, what are you hiding behind your back?

LOUIE   *(smiles and hands her a bouquet)*

             Just a little something for our golden anniversary,
             Josie.

JOSIE   Oh, Louie. My favorite flower...tulips! You remem-
             bered after all these years!

LOUIE   How could I forget? I brought you a bouquet of tu-
             lips the first time I showed up at your house to
             take you on a date.

JOSIE   And what a date it was! My dad grilled you like a
             police detective about where we were going, and he
             made you promise to have me home by ten.

LOUIE   Yes. And I gained points with your mother when I
             showed up with flowers.

JOSIE   Yes, Mom was just like me...sentimental. Fifty
             years! It seems like yesterday.

LOUIE   I have a confession to make.

JOSIE   What is it?

LOUIE   It's about the tulips. I picked them from a garden
             in the park on my way to your house.

JOSIE   *(laughs)*

             You what?

LOUIE *(nods and grins)*

I thought it was about time I admitted it to you. I've felt guilty for fifty years.

JOSIE *(laughs)*

And you should feel guilty!

(examines her bouquet)

And what about these? Are they from a church garden or somebody's backyard?

LOUIE No, Josie. I bought them at the florist when I went out earlier. And you know something? The color is perfect for a golden anniversary.

JOSIE Why, yes, that's right. They're yellow—gold.

(wipes her eyes)

Louie, you always were something!

LOUIE And I know a song that goes perfectly with the flowers.

(smiles, begins singing, and then motions for everybody to join in)

ALL *Tip-toe to the window, by the window,*
That's where I'll be.
Come tip-toe thru the tulips with me.

Tip-toe from your pillow to the shadow of a willow tree,
And tip-toe thru the tulips with me.

Knee deep, in flowers we'll stray.
We'll keep the showers away.

And if I kiss you in the garden,
In the moonlight,
Will you pardon me,
Come tip-toe thru the tulips with me.

(repeat)

The End

Other Books by Venture Publishing, Inc.

Experience Marketing: Strategies for the New Millennium
        by Ellen L. O'Sullivan and Kathy J. Spangler
Facilitation Techniques in Therapeutic Recreation
        by John Dattilo
File o' Fun: A Recreation Planner for Games & Activities, Third Edition
        by Jane Harris Ericson and Diane Ruth Albright
Functional Interdisciplinary-Transdisciplinary Therapy (FITT) Manual
        by Deborah M. Schott, Judy D. Burdett, Beverly J. Cook, Karren S. Ford, and Kathleen M. Orban
The Game and Play Leader's Handbook: Facilitating Fun and Positive Interaction, Revised Edition
        by Bill Michaelis and John M. O'Connell
The Game Finder—A Leader's Guide to Great Activities
        by Annette C. Moore
Getting People Involved in Life and Activities: Effective Motivating Techniques
        by Jeanne Adams
Glossary of Recreation Therapy and Occupational Therapy
        by David R. Austin
Great Special Events and Activities
        by Annie Morton, Angie Prosser, and Sue Spangler
Group Games & Activity Leadership
        by Kenneth J. Bulik
Growing With Care: Using Greenery, Gardens, and Nature With Aging and Special Populations
        by Betsy Kreidler
Hands On! Children's Activities for Fairs, Festivals, and Special Events
        by Karen L. Ramey
Health Promotion for Mind, Body and Spirit
        by Suzanne Fitzsimmons and Linda L. Buettner
In Search of the Starfish: Creating a Caring Environment
        by Mary Hart, Karen Primm, and Kathy Cranisky
Inclusion: Including People With Disabilities in Parks and Recreation Opportunities
        by Lynn Anderson and Carla Brown Kress
Inclusive Leisure Services: Responding to the Rights of People with Disabilities, Second Edition
        by John Dattilo
Innovations: A Recreation Therapy Approach to Restorative Programs
        by Dawn R. De Vries and Julie M. Lake
Internships in Recreation and Leisure Services: A Practical Guide for Students, Third Edition
        by Edward E. Seagle, Jr. and Ralph W. Smith
Interpretation of Cultural and Natural Resources, Second Edition
        by Douglas M. Knudson, Ted T. Cable, and Larry Beck
Intervention Activities for At-Risk Youth
        by Norma J. Stumbo
Introduction to Outdoor Recreation: Providing and Managing Resource Based Opportunities
        by Roger L. Moore and B.L. Driver
Introduction to Recreation and Leisure Services, Eighth Edition
        by Karla A. Henderson, M. Deborah Bialeschki, John L. Hemingway, Jan S. Hodges, Beth D. Kivel, and
        H. Douglas Sessoms
Introduction to Therapeutic Recreation: U.S. and Canadian Perspectives
        by Kenneth Mobily and Lisa Ostiguy
Introduction to Writing Goals and Objectives: A Manual for Recreation Therapy Students and Entry-Level
        Professionals
        by Suzanne Melcher
Leadership and Administration of Outdoor Pursuits, Second Edition
        by Phyllis Ford and James Blanchard
Leadership in Leisure Services: Making a Difference, Second Edition
        by Debra J. Jordan
Leisure Services in Canada: An Introduction, Second Edition
        by Mark S. Searle and Russell E. Brayley

Leisure and Leisure Services in the 21st Century: Toward Mid Century
        by Geoffrey Godbey
The Leisure Diagnostic Battery: Users Manual and Sample Forms
        by Peter A. Witt and Gary Ellis
Leisure Education I: A Manual of Activities and Resources, Second Edition
        by Norma J. Stumbo
Leisure Education II: More Activities and Resources, Second Edition
        by Norma J. Stumbo
Leisure Education III: More Goal-Oriented Activities
        by Norma J. Stumbo
Leisure Education IV: Activities for Individuals with Substance Addictions
        by Norma J. Stumbo
Leisure Education Program Planning: A Systematic Approach, Second Edition
        by John Dattilo
Leisure Education Specific Programs
        by John Dattilo
Leisure in Your Life: An Exploration, Sixth Edition
        by Geoffrey Godbey
Leisure Services in Canada: An Introduction, Second Edition
        by Mark S. Searle and Russell E. Brayley
Leisure Studies: Prospects for the Twenty-First Century
        edited by Edgar L. Jackson and Thomas L. Burton
The Lifestory Re-Play Circle: A Manual of Activities and Techniques
        by Rosilyn Wilder
Marketing in Leisure and Tourism: Reaching New Heights
        by Patricia Click Janes
The Melody Lingers On: A Complete Music Activities Program for Older Adults
        by Bill Messenger
Models of Change in Municipal Parks and Recreation: A Book of Innovative Case Studies
        edited by Mark E. Havitz
More Than a Game: A New Focus on Senior Activity Services
        by Brenda Corbett
The Multiple Values of Wilderness
        by H. Ken Cordell, John C. Bergstrom, and J.M. Bowker
Nature and the Human Spirit: Toward an Expanded Land Management Ethic
        edited by B.L. Driver, Daniel Dustin, Tony Baltic, Gary Elsner, and George Peterson
The Organizational Basis of Leisure Participation: A Motivational Exploration
        by Robert A. Stebbins
Outdoor Recreation for 21st Century America
        by H. Ken Cordell
Outdoor Recreation Management: Theory and Application, Third Edition
        by Alan Jubenville and Ben Twight
Planning and Organizing Group Activities in Social Recreation
        by John V. Valentine
Planning Parks for People, Second Edition
        by John Hultsman, Richard L. Cottrell, and Wendy Z. Hultsman
The Process of Recreation Programming Theory and Technique, Third Edition
        by Patricia Farrell and Herberta M. Lundegren
Programming for Parks, Recreation, and Leisure Services: A Servant Leadership Approach, Second Edition
        by Debra J. Jordan, Donald G. DeGraaf, and Kathy H. DeGraaf
Protocols for Recreation Therapy Programs
        edited by Jill Kelland, along with the Recreation Therapy Staff at Alberta Hospital Edmonton
Puttin' on the Skits: Plays for Adults in Managed Care
        by Jean Vetter
Quality Management: Applications for Therapeutic Recreation
        edited by Bob Riley

A Recovery Workbook: The Road Back from Substance Abuse
        by April K. Neal and Michael J. Taleff
Recreation and Leisure: Issues in an Era of Change, Third Edition
        edited by Thomas Goodale and Peter A. Witt
Recreation and Youth Development
        by Peter A. Witt and Linda L. Caldwell
Recreation Economic Decisions: Comparing Benefits and Costs, Second Edition
        by John B. Loomis and Richard G. Walsh
Recreation for Older Adults: Individual and Group Activities
        by Judith A. Elliott and Jerold E. Elliott
Recreation Program Planning Manual for Older Adults
        by Karen Kindrachuk
Recreation Programming and Activities for Older Adults
        by Jerold E. Elliott and Judith A. Sorg-Elliott
Reference Manual for Writing Rehabilitation Therapy Treatment Plans
        by Penny Hogberg and Mary Johnson
Research in Therapeutic Recreation: Concepts and Methods
        edited by Marjorie J. Malkin and Christine Z. Howe
Simple Expressions: Creative and Therapeutic Arts for the Elderly in Long-Term Care Facilities
        by Vicki Parsons
A Social History of Leisure Since 1600
        by Gary Cross
A Social Psychology of Leisure
        by Roger C. Mannell and Douglas A. Kleiber
Special Events and Festivals: How to Organize, Plan, and Implement
        by Angie Prosser and Ashli Rutledge
Stretch Your Mind and Body: Tai Chi as an Adaptive Activity
        by Duane A. Crider and William R. Klinger
Therapeutic Activity Intervention with the Elderly: Foundations and Practices
        by Barbara A. Hawkins, Marti E. May, and Nancy Brattain Rogers
Therapeutic Recreation and the Nature of Disabilities
        by Kenneth E. Mobily and Richard D. MacNeil
Therapeutic Recreation: Cases and Exercises, Second Edition
        by Barbara C. Wilhite and M. Jean Keller
Therapeutic Recreation in Health Promotion and Rehabilitation
        by John Shank and Catherine Coyle
Therapeutic Recreation in the Nursing Home
        by Linda Buettner and Shelley L. Martin
Therapeutic Recreation Programming: Theory and Practice
        by Charles Sylvester, Judith E. Voelkl, and Gary D. Ellis
Therapeutic Recreation Protocol for Treatment of Substance Addictions
        by Rozanne W. Faulkner
The Therapeutic Recreation Stress Management Primer
        by Cynthia Mascott
The Therapeutic Value of Creative Writing
        by Paul M. Spicer
Tourism and Society: A Guide to Problems and Issues
        by Robert W. Wyllie
Traditions: Improving Quality of Life in Caregiving
        by Janelle Sellick

Venture Publishing, Inc.
1999 Cato Avenue
State College, PA 16801
Phone: 814-234-4561
Fax: 814-234-1651